DATE DUE			

TRACKS
ACROSS AMERICA

TRACKS ACROSS AMERICA

The Story of the American Railroad 1825–1900

with photographs, maps, and drawings

LEONARD EVERETT FISHER

Holiday House / New York

ACKNOWLEDGMENTS

I wish to thank the following institutions for permission to reprint the pictorial material in this book: Association of American Railroads (pages 29, 30, 150–151, 173); Brown Brothers (163); Buffalo Bill Historical Center (109); Chicago Historical Society (68–69); Culver Pictures, Inc. (76, 116, 130); DeGolyer Library, Southern Methodist University (98–99, 184); Denver Public Library (119); The Historic Pullman Foundation (174); Illinois State Historical Library (44); International Museum of Photography, George Eastman House (159); Kansas State Historical Society (93, 106); Library of Congress (jacket, 11, 36–37, 39, 46, 51, 55, 58, 59, 60, 62–63, 67, 71, 73, 76, 88–89, 91, 94–95, 107, 122, 132, 153, 155, 166, 175); Mansell Collection, London, England (15); Minnesota Historical Society (137); Montana Historical Society (145); National Archives (54, 65, 83, 102, 111); National Gallery of Art (40–41); New York Historical Society (32–33, 131, 135); New York Public Library (125, 160); Oakland Museum History Dept. (149); Oklahoma State Historical Society (112); Oregon Historical Society (146–147); Putnam Museum (45); Science Museum, London, England (13, 24, 25); Smithsonian Institution (16, 28, 101, 141, 143, 167); Southern Pacific Railroad (77, 86, 87); Union Pacific Railroad Museum (2, 134, 172); University of Iowa (43); University of Michigan Library (17); Van Pelt-Dietrich Library, University of Pennsylvania (49, 53); Westinghouse Electric Corporation (179); S.C. Williams Library, Stevens Institute of Technology (19, 20).

L.E.F.

Library of Congress Cataloging-in-Publication Data
Fisher, Leonard Everett.
Tracks across America : the story of the American railroad,
1825–1900 / Leonard Everett Fisher.
p.   cm.
Includes bibliographical references.
Summary: Examines the development of the railroad in the
United States from its nineteenth-century beginnings to the
end of that century.
ISBN 0-8234-0945-7
1. Railroads—United States—History—Juvenile literature.
[1. Railroads—History.] I. Title.
TF23.F58   1992   91-28244   CIP   AC
385′.0973—dc20

O the engineer's joys! to go with a locomotive!
To hear the hiss of steam, the merry shriek, the steam-whistle,
the laughing locomotive!

Walt Whitman,
"Song of Joys,"
1860

Also by Leonard Everett Fisher

Nonfiction

The Alamo
Ellis Island
Monticello
The Oregon Trail
The Statue of Liberty
The White House

Picture Books

Cyclops
Jason and the Golden Fleece
The Olympians: Great Gods and Goddesses of Ancient Greece
The Seven Days of Creation
Theseus and the Minotaur

Contents

Map of the eastern part of the United States, 1825
LEONARD EVERETT FISHER

1.

Before the Iron Horse

Between 1800 and 1825, the principal arteries of travel in America were dirt roads and natural waterways. Raw materials from the West, like lumber, traveled to the Atlantic coastal communities by horse and wagon, river ferries, and small boats. East Coast businessmen who needed raw materials to manufacture their products were frustrated by the high cost of such slow transportation. Goods that Easterners manufactured from western raw materials, like furniture, took just as long to reach the western frontier from the East.

Between the East and the West lay the Mississippi River, flowing south into smaller rivers, making the Mississippi a great north-south trade area. Between the East Coast and the Mississippi lay the Appalachian mountain range, which made east-west overland shipments slow and costly. The businessmen on the East Coast wanted to find a way to cut the high cost of shipping and to speed up and increase the east-west flow of trade by eliminating the Mississippi River network and mountainous overland routes. They took note that France and England were crisscrossed with a system of barge canals—artificial waterways—that had been moving commercial goods and passengers since about 1700. And so canals were dug in Pennsylvania, New York, and elsewhere. Through these canals passed an endless stream of barges laden with goods and passengers. The barges were attached to horses or mules, which walked along the bank on either side of the canal, pulling the barge forward.

In 1825, what had been a noisy, grinding three-week wagon trip from Buffalo to Albany, New York, became a quiet, leisurely one-week barge trip on the newly completed Erie Canal, a 40-foot-wide, four-foot-deep waterway nicknamed "the Big Ditch." The 360-mile canal connected Lake Erie with the Hudson River, the Great Lakes with the Atlantic Ocean, and the western United States with the eastern United States. The shipment of raw materials from the West via the Great Lakes to Buffalo, through the Erie Canal to Albany, and then south via the Hudson River to New York City was faster and less costly than it had been on roads and natural waterways. Freight charges, which had been as high as $100 a ton, dropped dramatically to $20 a ton, and even further to $5 a ton within the first 10 years of the Erie Canal operation. The new route made the East the manufacturing center of the country. Thanks to the Erie Canal and its horse-drawn barges, New York City became at once a commercial hub, the financial capital of the entire nation, and America's largest, most active deepwater port. Canal workers proudly sang:

"Attend all ye drivers, I sing of my team;
They're the fleetest and strongest that ever was seen . . .
The three altogether in motion outdo
Any team of their age, the whole canal through."

In their enthusiasm to move the canal projects forward, no one had given serious thought to harnessing steam power instead of using horses to transport barges of material and passengers. Horses had been around forever. A tired old horse pulling a coal- or iron-laden cart out of a mine along

Horse-drawn barge on the Erie Canal, 1819
LIBRARY OF CONGRESS

smooth wood rails was not an unfamiliar sight in England, continental Europe, or America.

More than 2,000 years ago, the ancient Greeks constructed wood rails on crude roads to ease the hauling of heavy wagons by oxen, horses, and humans. In the mid-1500s, horses started pulling wagons and carts along wood rails ("wagonways," "tramways," or "rail-roads") in continental Europe and England. Smooth wood tracks made it easier for the horses to haul carts out of the mines. During the 1700s, strips of brittle cast iron were laid over the tops of the wood rails to keep them from wearing out. These tracks were called strap rails. Later, the cast-iron strips were replaced by stronger, wrought-iron strips. All-iron rails were cast in England as early as 1767 but did not come into general use until 1810, when a few began to replace wood rails. Still, no one had yet addressed replacing horses with a steam engine.

The earliest-known steam engine was invented in ancient Egypt about 2,100 years ago. The Egyptians boiled a kettle of water over a wood fire. The hot, damp steam was channeled into a hollow ball through pipes. A couple of bent tubes also pierced the ball. Hissing steam escaped through the bent tubes, making the ball spin. It was a gadget that no one knew what to do with.

It took a little more than another 1,800 years before Captain Thomas Savery, an English army officer, came up with the idea to use steam to generate power in a useful way. In 1698, Savery built a steam engine to pump water out of a coal mine—to "raise water by fire," as he described its purpose. He called his engine the *Miner's Friend*. It was a pipe-like contraption that used steam and cold water to create a vacuum. The bottom end of the pipe sucked up the mine water, which then came out of the pipe's top end in a trickle. Savery compared the work of his steam engine to that of a horse and coined the term "horsepower."

Another Englishman, Thomas Newcomen, improved on Savery's steam-driven mine pump in 1712—but not by much. Newcomen's huge and clumsy *Atmospheric Engine* used great amounts of burning coal to heat water for steam to operate a pump. The steam pressure drove the pump by moving pistons enclosed in cylinders. There wasn't much pressure in Newcomen's steam engine. It drew the water out of the mine in a feeble stream.

Fifty-seven years later, in 1769, a Scottish instrument maker, James Watt, designed a more efficient low-pressure steam engine that used less coal, was a bit more powerful, and drew from the mine a little more water than previous pumps. But by 1800 an improved Watts steam engine could do many more things than drive water pumps. It could operate at different speeds by the use of a throttle. And with an attached crankshaft it was strong enough to turn wheels. William Murdock, an employee of Watt, used the idea to construct a self-moving engine.

Newcomen steam engine, 1712
SCIENCE MUSEUM, LONDON, ENGLAND

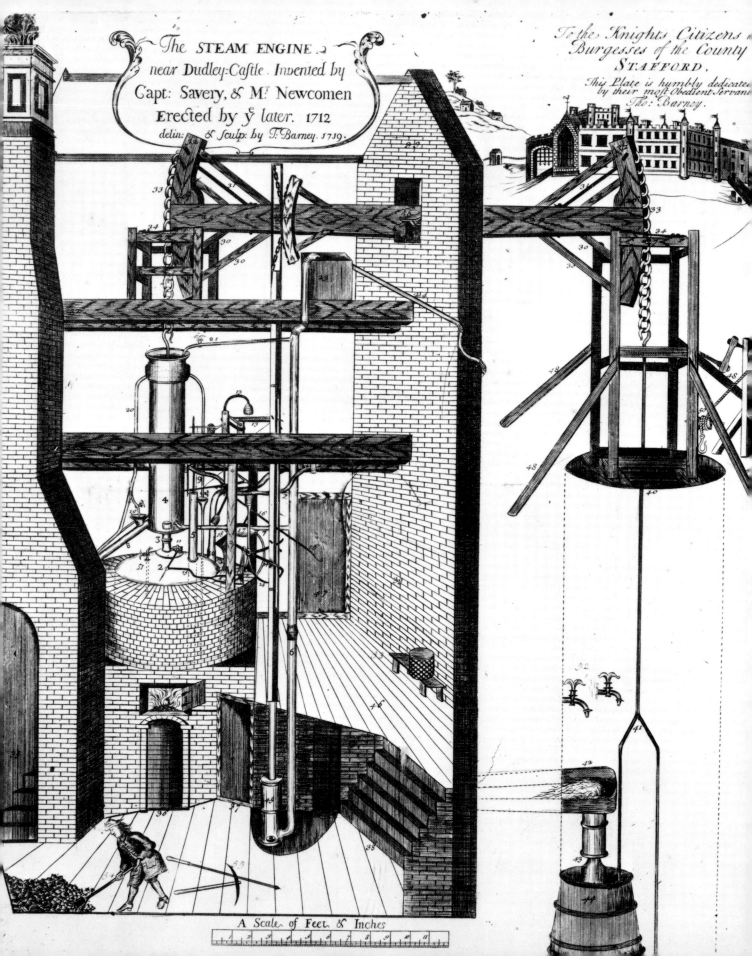

The STEAM ENGINE near Dudley-Castle. Invented by Capt: Savery, & Mr. Newcomen Erected by ye later. 1712

delin: & sculp: by T. Barney. 1719.

To the Knights Citizens & Burgesses of the County of STAFFORD,

This Plate is humbly dedicated by their most Obedient Servant Tho: Barney.

A Scale of Feet & Inches

2.

The First Railroads

In 1800, an iron-mine mechanic in the southwest of England, Richard Trevithick, saw the possibility of linking the Watt-Murdock throttle-controlled steam engine to a horseless wagon. He built a small, compact high-pressure steam engine of his own, constructed a carriage around it, called it *Captain Dick's Puffer*, and ran it through the streets without the aid of horses or any other means of locomotion.

In 1804, Trevithick designed a small, steam-powered machine on wheels for Nicholas Humphrey, owner of the Pennydarran Iron Works at Merthyr Tydfil in South Wales. A competitor had bet Humphrey that he could not move a load of iron on a nine-mile strap-rail tramway from the ironworks to a dock without the aid of horses or men. Trevithick's engine, first called *Tram Engine* and then *Trevithick's Portable Steam Engine*, easily hauled 10 tons of iron and some 70 people in five wagons when it was on track. But on its way the heavy machine slipped off the rail and toppled into a ditch. Righted by a team of horses each time it derailed, it was set on its way again at five miles an hour and won the day—and Humphrey's bet.

Humphrey lost interest in the engine, however, when his wagon masters complained about the locomotive's threat to their livelihood—horse-drawn carts and wagons. Regardless of its indifferent treatment, *Trevithick's Portable Steam*

Richard Trevithick
MANSELL COLLECTION, LONDON, ENGLAND

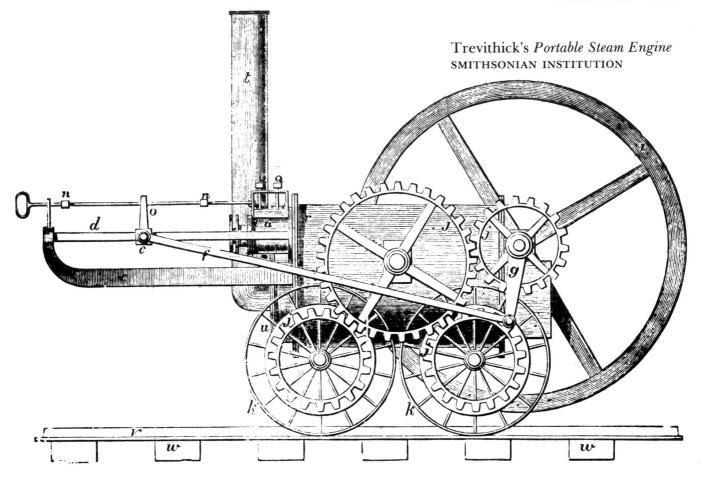

Trevithick's *Portable Steam Engine*
SMITHSONIAN INSTITUTION

Engine was the first workable self-propelled locomotive to haul carts along a railway.

In 1808, Trevithick took his locomotive to London, renamed the engine *Catch Me Who Can*, and charged admission to see it run. Huge crowds came to watch the marvelous machine puff its way around a fenced-in circular track. When the engine was wrecked in a derailment, the people stopped coming. Disheartened, Trevithick, the Father of the Locomotive, returned to the mines. In 1816, he moved to South America, where he thought he could create more interest in his locomotive. He died a pauper.

While Trevithick was building his locomotive in South Wales, Oliver Evans, a Wilmington, Delaware, mechanical genius, was tinkering with a vastly improved high-pressure steam engine. In 1760, at the age of 25, Evans had designed the first automatic water-powered mill in the world. Instead of using workers to stir, grind, and carry the grain, he invented the elevator, a conveyor belt, and an automatic grain mixer to do the jobs. People thought he was mad, laughed at him, and convinced themselves that there was little or no future to his weird engines.

In 1804, unaware of Trevithick and having only read about Newcomen's big and clumsy steam engine pump, Oliver Evans designed a much smaller steam engine that could grind grain, saw timber, cut marble, drive a boat, and even drive a carriage. In that year, 1804, he unveiled a peculiar-looking steam-driven dredge, a wheeled machine to scrape and deepen the bottom of Philadelphia's Schuylkill River. The self-propelled 30-foot-long, 15-ton vehicle was called the *Orukter Amphibolos*, the "amphibious digger." Its five-horsepower steam engine made it the first successful high-pressure steam vehicle in America to move under its own power. It was also the first amphibious vehicle in the world.

Oliver Evans badgered potential backers to provide him

Oliver Evans' *Orukter Amphibolos*
UNIVERSITY OF MICHIGAN LIBRARY

with funds to build a steam-driven carriage and run it on rails at about 15 miles an hour between New York and Philadelphia. The backers thought he was crazy. He died in 1819, less than 10 years before steam-driven railroads would appear in America, but not before writing of the future as he saw it:

> The time will come when people will travel in stages moved by steam engines, from one city to another . . . [at] fifteen to twenty miles an hour. . . . I do verily believe that carriages propelled by steam will come into general use, and travel at the rate of 300 miles a day.

Another nineteenth-century railroad enthusiast, a lawyer named John Latrobe, who represented the Baltimore & Ohio Railroad during its first 50 years, wrote:

> In the beginning no one dreamed of steam upon the road. Horses were to do the work. . . . Relays of horses trotted the cars from place to place . . . thundering along, the roll of the wheels on the combined rail of stone and iron being almost deafening.

Only a few visionaries like Oliver Evans considered hauling goods and people everywhere around the nation with a steam engine on wheels. John Stevens, a New York aristocrat, businessman, and lawyer with engineering talents, predicted such an engine would one day travel at a "velocity of 100 miles an hour."

Stevens belonged to a wealthy landholding family who sided with the British during the American Revolution. He threw in his lot, however, with the rebellious colonists. Stevens summered in Hoboken, New Jersey, and practiced a little law. He dreamed of building a tunnel under the

John Stevens
STEVENS INSTITUTE

18

Hudson River between New York and New Jersey. He spent his time designing efficient high-pressure steam engines that could power propeller-driven boats and possibly pull wagons on rails. His vision was to make a practical, profitable steam engine. He was a businessman at heart and hired skilled mechanics to build that vision into reality. By 1800, he had a lively business of ferrying passengers across the Hudson River from New York to a fashionable Hoboken picnic ground, the Elysian Fields. He used steamboats of his design with two propellers that traveled at three to four miles an hour. And to demonstrate his point about the possibility of steam-powered railroads, Stevens built a steam locomotive in 1825 and ran it on a circular track on his summer estate in Hoboken.

John Stevens's son, Robert Livingston Stevens, would make a lasting contribution to the mechanics of the railroad. Robert L. was president of the Camden & Amboy

Stevens's steam locomotive, Hoboken, New Jersey, 1825
STEVENS INSTITUTE

Railroad, which ran between Philadelphia and New York City. In 1830, while on a ship bound for England, where he intended to buy some railroad equipment, he designed a radically different type of rail than the three-foot-long strap rails that were then in common use. His all-wrought-iron rail was called a T rail. When a deeply flanged wheel rode on it, there would be less chance that a locomotive or car would slip off the track. Some earlier rails had a lip or flange on them to keep the locomotive wheels on track, but they were practically useless. The weight of the engines flattened and crushed the flanges, wearing the rails smooth again.

Stevens designed his rail in 16-foot lengths to be laid on granite blocks set into the earth. Being impatient to test his new rails, he spiked them to squared-off wood logs tied perpendicularly—crosstied—to the rails on a crushed-rock roadway. These crossties were called sleepers. Much to his

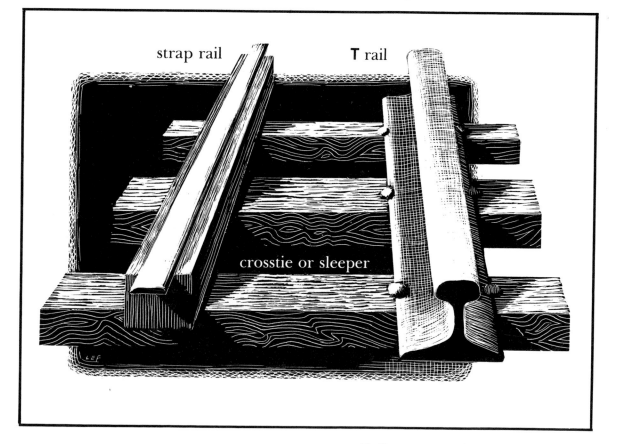

Rail types
LEONARD EVERETT FISHER

surprise, the ride over these rails was more flexible and smoother than the jarring, rocking ride provided by the strap-rail track laid over immovable granite blocks. By 1840, there were about 5,000 miles of railroad track in the United States. And by 1840, the T rail and its method of being set on the ground had quickly become the standard equipment and system used all over the world, the model for all modern railroad tracks. In about 1860, some iron rails were replaced by steel rails by the Pennsylvania Railroad. By 1900, nearly every mile of the 200,000 miles of iron T rails in America would be replaced by stronger steel T rails.

By 1825, the application of civil and mechanical engineering to railroads had become a well-developed science. Although the machinery was small, quaint, and often clumsy, the underlying theoretical and practical mathematics used to construct steam locomotives, high-pressure steam boilers, and devices for laying tracks was sophisticated enough to transform a whole society. In that year, 1825, a British civil engineer, Thomas Tredgold, a member of the Institution of Civil Engineers, published the first treatise on "rail-road" design—"Showing the Principles of Estimating . . . the Theory, Effect, and Expense of Steam Carriages, Stationary Engines, and Gas Machines."

During this period, 1823–1825, George Stephenson, a British expert on steam-driven coal-mine pumps and winding and lifting machinery, built a steam locomotive for his company. He was a mechanical engineer for the Stockton & Darlington Railway in northern England. It had received a royal charter in 1821 to build a public tramway "for hauling wagons and other carriages" by means of "men or horses or otherwise."

There was nothing new about public tramways. In 1803, public strap-rail tracks were laid in Surrey, England, to bring Surrey's farm products to London markets. Anyone could use the tracks. There were no train schedules. In fact, there were no trains, just farmers driving horse-drawn wagons of vegetables, fruits, and animals along the tracks. The only requirement to use the tracks was that the farmer had to provide his own horse and wagon.

By 1800, the Industrial Age was upon England and the world. The change in productivity—from a centuries-old agricultural society to an industrial economy—demanded a cheaper, speedier, and more efficient means of bringing farm and industrial products to market. The owners of the Stockton & Darlington Railway knew that the best means of doing this was described in their charter as "otherwise," meaning steam-powered locomotion. Stephenson agreed.

Stephenson had studied the innovative steam locomotives built by John Blenkinsop and William Hedley, coal-mine engineers. Blenkinsop's contribution to the locomotive was his design of a wheel system that fit into rack gears attached to the rails to keep the engine from running off the track. Blenkinsop's engine with Hedley's two locomotives, the *Wylam Dilly* and *Puffing Billy*, influenced Stephenson's design for his first steam locomotive, the *Blücher*, built in 1814 for the Killingworth coal-mine tramway. Stephenson thought he could design an improved engine and was given the job. The locomotive itself was to be built in the Newcastle workshops of Robert Stephenson and Company, managed by his brother. His own son, Robert, was a partner in the company.

On September 27, 1825, Stephenson's *Locomotion No. 1* successfully pulled 30 cars loaded with water, coal, flour, and people at seven or eight miles an hour along an 18-mile stretch of track in northern England. The age of transporting freight by rail over long distances had begun. America was not far behind.

Five years later, on September 15, 1830, the first steam-

Rack Locomotive
SCIENCE MUSEUM, LONDON, ENGLAND

powered public rail passenger service in the world—the Liverpool & Manchester Railway—opened in England. The Liverpool & Manchester was originally built to give farmers and manufacturers of the Manchester area a way to transport their produce and goods to the port city of Liverpool. The company had no thought of a steam-powered railway. Horse-drawn cars, or even a horse working a treadmill inside a car to propel its wheels, were suggested as a means of rail power. Urged on by George Stephenson to adopt steam power, the company decided to hold a competition for the best locomotive.

Four locomotives were entered, among them George and Robert Stephenson's *Rocket*. The contestants had to meet certain standards for cost, safety, weight, ability to haul heavy cargoes at certain speeds, and speed with light cargo.

The only engine that qualified was the *Rocket*. The others broke down, and one even exploded before it got under

The *Wylam Dilly*
SCIENCE MUSEUM, LONDON, ENGLAND

way. But the success of the Stephensons' *Rocket*—which could fly along the rails at 29 miles an hour—in meeting all the conditions of the competition determined the type of power for the Liverpool & Manchester Railway.

The farmers and landowners of the area loudly objected to an "iron horse" roaring through their district, upsetting the cows and chickens, setting fire to the haystacks, and polluting the air with soot and noise. Their protests fell on the deaf ears of those powerful interests determined to achieve steam rail power.

Eight cars filled with 800 important and fashionable passengers left Liverpool for Manchester in a pouring rain that September 15, pulled by the locomotive *Northumbrian*, another Stephenson-built locomotive. The cars were nothing more than the familiar stagecoaches put on "trucks," or railroad wheels to fit the track width. The prime minister himself, the Duke of Wellington—the hero of the Battle of Waterloo who defeated Napoleon Bonaparte—was aboard the lead car to celebrate the event. By the end of the year, the Liverpool & Manchester Railway had transported 70,000 passengers.

"The engine was set off at its utmost speed . . . swifter than a bird flies," wrote Fanny Kemble, a passenger aboard the Northumbrian. "You cannot conceive what a sensation of cutting the air was; the motion as smooth as possible too. I stood up, and with my bonnet off drank the air before me." The Railway Age, the Age of the Common Carrier— the "common carrier" being any company that transports passengers and freight for payment—had begun in earnest.

Two years before, in 1828, Horatio Allen, an American civil engineer and graduate of Columbia University who had helped design the Erie Canal, was sent to England by the Delaware & Hudson Canal Company to study the successful use of steam locomotives on coal-mine railways. By this time, English steam locomotives had begun to replace horses on many strap-rail tramways throughout the country. The Delaware & Hudson Canal Company, for whom Allen now worked, owned coal mines in Carbondale, Pennsylvania. It constructed its own 16-mile railway to haul coal to Honesdale in horse-drawn wagons. There, by means of a company-owned canal system, the coal was shipped to the Hudson River. The company was anxious to improve its transport system. Horses were too slow and expensive to maintain. The company wanted to replace horses on the coal-mine railway with faster, cheaper power. Allen was so convinced that the British steam locomotive was the answer that he had four of them loaded onto a ship and brought to America.

On August 8, 1829, four years after the opening of the Erie Canal, in a quiet corner of northeastern Pennsylvania, Horatio Allen drove one of these British steam locomotives, the seven-ton *Stourbridge Lion*, along the 16-mile track from Honesdale to Carbondale. Years later, Allen remarked: "On this first movement by steam on railroad in this continent, I was engineer, fireman, brakeman, conductor, and passenger."

Over the next few years railroads with steam-powered locomotives instead of horse power began to appear in various parts of the East, North, and South. Their tracks usually followed the canals and rivers that were used for so much of commercial traffic. Although there was excitement about the new machinery on wheels, there was also resistance to change.

America had always been a farming country. Now, 50 years after ending its British colonial status, the United States had begun to transform itself from an agricultural society into a mighty industrial nation. The days of pastoral quiet and clean air were slowly fading. The smoky smell

The *Stourbridge Lion*
SMITHSONIAN INSTITUTION

and metallic clank of industrial progress was beginning to emerge. The United States was becoming a different place from the one it had been when it won its independence. And there were many who felt uneasy about change. The railroad was not only something of a symbol of that change but an instrument for change as well. The railroads would create a different life for those near the new lines. And some places, once thriving but soon to be out of reach of the railroads, would be facing harder times.

A few businessmen in Charleston, South Carolina, realizing the possible importance of a railway that could transport their large cotton crop to market, formed the South Carolina Canal & Railway Company in 1827. In 1830, they built a strap-rail track between Charleston and Hamburg and ran a train between the two cities. The train was pulled either by a horse or by a sail car. The sail car, which was nothing more than a boxlike sailboat on wheels, needed a

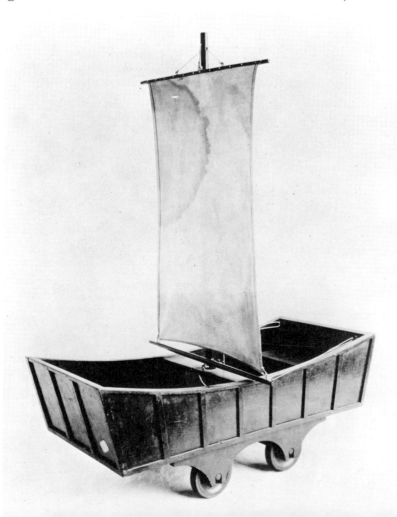

Sail car
ASSOCIATION OF
AMERICAN RAILROADS

strong wind at its rear to move it forward. If there was no wind, the sail car remained motionless. One wind was so strong it tore the sail from its mast and rendered the sail car useless. The technique proved to be ridiculous and impractical. The Charleston group then hired Horatio Allen, who had recently introduced the English steam locomotive to the Pennsylvania coalfields, to build a steam locomotive. Allen in turn hired a New York foundry to do the job.

The locomotive, the first ever built in America and called the *Best Friend of Charleston*, went into service on December 25, 1830. The engine was built at the West Point Foundry in New York. For six months it hauled passengers and freight back and forth between Charleston and Hamburg at speeds of about 20 miles per hour. It hauled freight at night, too, lighting up the tracks with a fire on a flatcar pushed by the locomotive. In June 1831 it blew up, killing the crewman who mistakenly shut down a pressure valve. For a number of years following the disaster, railroad promoters had a difficult time convincing a frightened public that railroads using steam locomotives were safe, provided a good alternative to canals and stagecoaches, and were here to stay.

Farther north, in New York State, the 17-mile-long Albany to Schenectady Mohawk & Hudson Railway put its first locomotive-drawn train in service. On a steamy August morning in 1831, a 12-foot-long, 6,750-pound engine chugged down the rails lined by a huge throng. The engine's name was the *De Witt Clinton*. It was named for the governor of New York who built the Erie Canal. Like the *Best Friend of Charleston*, the *De Witt Clinton* was built at the West Point Foundry. The locomotive had three carriages and six flatcars loaded with festive passengers. Partway into

the run, the belching smokestack sent sooty smoke that all but hid the train from view. Worse still, the passengers were assaulted by red-hot embers that set their clothes on fire. As luck would have it, no one was seriously injured as the train pulled up to a stop to take on water. There the smoldering passengers drenched themselves with water and reboarded the train to complete the short ride, still fighting off the smoke and embers.

J. L. Gillis, a Philadelphia judge, recalled his smoke-choked fiery trip on that historic day:

> The train was composed of coach bodies . . . placed upon trucks. The trucks were coupled together with chains, leaving from two to three feet slack, and when the locomotive started it took up the slack by jerks, with sufficient force to jerk the passengers who sat on seats across the tops of the coaches, out from under their hats, and in stopping, came together with such force as to send them flying from their seats. . . . There being no smoke or spark catcher to the chimney . . . a volume of black smoke, strongly impregnated with sparks, coals, and cinders, came pouring back the whole length of the train. Each of the tossed passengers who had an umbrella raised it as a protection against the smoke and fire. . . . I think in the first mile the last umbrella went overboard, all having their covers burnt off. . . . A general mêlée took place among the deck passengers, each whipping his neighbor to put out the fire. They presented a very motley appearance on arriving at the first station.

In 1833, rails were used to haul stone out of a North Carolina quarry on flatcars drawn by mules. The one-and-a-quarter-mile track ran from the quarry to the site of the

The *Best Friend of Charleston*
ASSOCIATION OF AMERICAN RAILROADS

capitol building then under construction in Raleigh. Three years later there were two railroads in North Carolina, the Wilmington & Weldon and the Raleigh & Gaston. By 1840 the Wilmington & Weldon, 161 miles long, had become the world's longest railroad.

Local laws were passed to prevent railroad companies from building their lines through towns that did not want them. Usually, these laws were brought about by politically powerful innkeepers, tavern owners, and other small businessmen who depended on stagecoach owners and drivers and barge canal users for their economic well-being. They would always call attention to the 1831 *Best Friend of Charleston* tragedy. On occasion, civil engineers surveying land tracts for railroad routes were run off by sharpshooters who objected to the coming of the railroad. In some areas where short lines managed to operate, local gangs tore up tracks and snipers fired shots at engine crews. Once in a while, a

The race between the *Tom Thumb* and a horse-drawn railcar, August 28, 1830
NEW YORK HISTORICAL SOCIETY

train was permitted to run on Sunday if church services were scheduled on board.

On August 25, 1830, a few months before the *Best Friend of Charleston* was put into service, the Baltimore & Ohio Railroad tested a small steam locomotive designed by a New Yorker named Peter Cooper. The engine was so small—one horsepower and one ton—that it was named *Tom Thumb*, after the miniature storybook character.

"The trip was most interesting," noted John Latrobe, the Baltimore & Ohio's lawyer. "The curves were passed without difficulty at a speed of fifteen miles an hour. . . . Some excited gentlemen . . . pulled out memorandum books . . . at the highest speed, which was eighteen miles an hour, wrote their names . . . to prove that even at that great velocity it was possible to do so."

The B & O had been founded by Baltimore merchants in 1827, the same year the South Carolina Canal & Railway

Company was chartered. Like the Charleston businessmen, the Baltimore group had business problems. The two-year-old Erie Canal in New York had effectively cut into their trade with Ohio. Baltimore merchants decided to lay their tracks straight into Ohio and to compete with the trade on the Erie Canal. They hoped to recapture some of their lost business.

Until the trial run of the *Tom Thumb*, the 13 miles of B & O track were devoted to horse-drawn cars. But on its trial run, the tiny locomotive proved that it could easily pull a passenger car with less wear and tear than a horse could. Horses on that line had to be changed at a halfway point some seven miles down the track. The *Tom Thumb* needed no rest or changeover. On its return trip, however, having made the first test of 13 miles successfully, the small engine with its attached passenger car was challenged at the halfway point by a horse-drawn car on the opposite track. Racing toward the finish, the locomotive pulled ahead of the horse. Unfortunately, a mechanical failure caused the engine to lose power and the race. But the engineers on board the locomotive had seen enough. They and company officials were convinced that with certain refinements, the iron horse would soon replace the real horse on railways and other public conveyances.

In 1851, Horatio Allen described for a crowd assembled at the opening of the New York & Erie Railroad his vision of "a thousand iron horses starting forth from the various railroad centers . . . traversing the continent in all directions."

3.

Going West

The fear of railroads began to wane. Rail lines sprouted all over the East. By 1835 at least a thousand miles of track had been laid. Boston itself had three separate lines that were beginning to reach out toward the rest of the country. The Baltimore & Ohio opened a branch line from Baltimore to Washington, D.C., and opened the first rail station in the world, the Mount Clare Depot. The B & O also extended its line to Harpers Ferry, Virginia.

Charles Dickens, the well-known English author of *Oliver Twist* and other novels dealing with the seamy side of British industrialization, toured the eastern United States in 1842. In volume 1 of his two-volume diary of the trip, *American Notes,* he complained about a rail trip he took between Boston and Lowell, Massachusetts, a factory town:

There are no first and second class carriages as with us; but there is a gentlemen's car and a ladies' car: the main distinction between which is that in the first, everybody smokes; and in the second, nobody does. As a black man never travels with a white one, there is also a negro car; which is a great blundering clumsy chest. . . . There is a great deal of jolting, a great deal of noise, a great deal of wall, not much window, a locomotive engine, a shriek, and a bell. . . . The cars are like shabby omnibusses. . . . In the center of the carriage there is usually

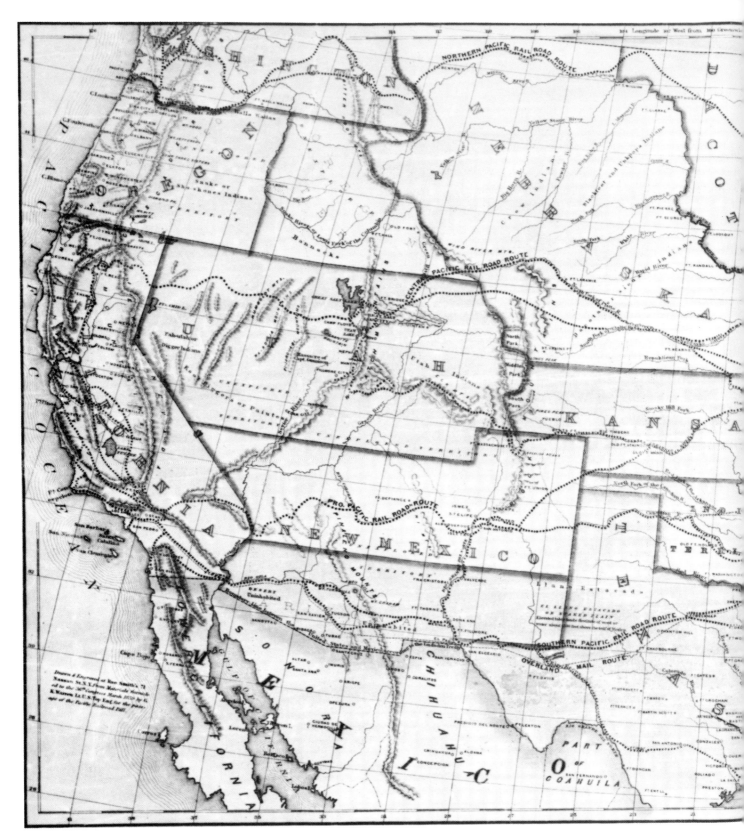

Railroad map of the United States, 1859
LIBRARY OF CONGRESS

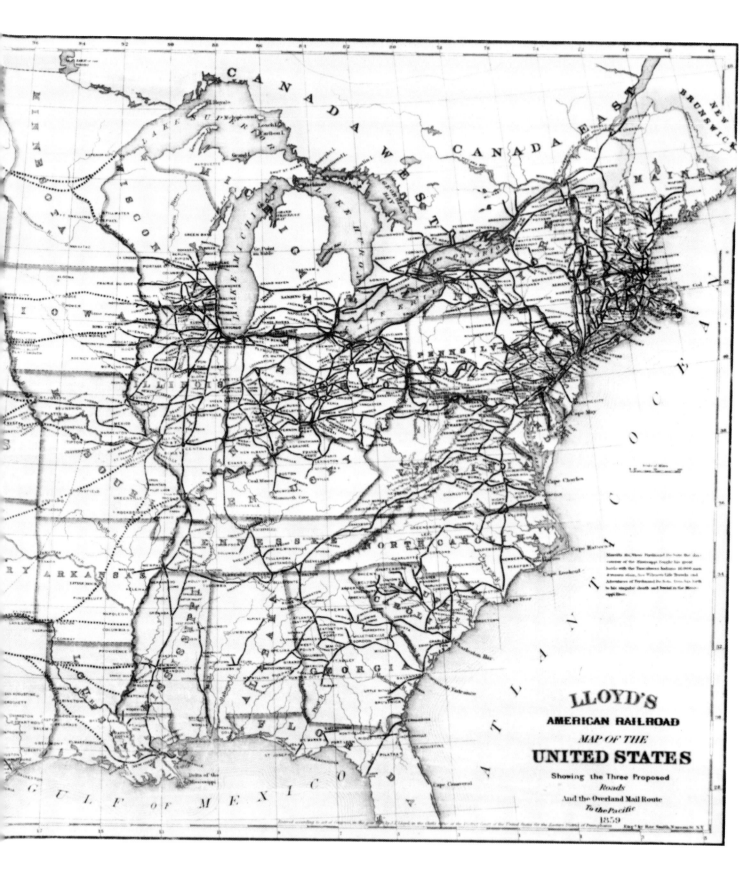

LLOYD'S
AMERICAN RAILROAD
MAP OF THE
UNITED STATES

Showing the Three Proposed
Roads
And the Overland Mail Route
To the Pacific
1859

a stove . . . insufferably close. . . . The train calls at stations in the woods, where the wild impossibility of anybody having the smallest reason to get out, is only equalled by the apparently desperate hopelessness of there being anybody to get in. . . . It rushes across the turnpike road, where there is no gate, no policeman, no signal: nothing but a rough wooden arch, on which is painted "WHEN THE BELL RINGS, LOOK OUT FOR THE LOCOMOTIVE." On it whirls headlong . . . on, on, on tears the mad dragon of an engine with its train of cars; scattering in all directions a shower of burning sparks from its wood fire; screeching, hissing, yelling, panting; until at last the thirsty monster stops between a covered way to drink, the people cluster around, and you have time to breathe again.

I returned at night by the same railroad and in the same kind of car. . . . I found abundance of entertainment for the rest of the ride in watching the effects of the wood fire, which had been invisible in the morning but were now brought out in full relief by the darkness: for we were travelling in a whirlwind of bright sparks, which showered about us like a storm of fiery snow.

In his 1844 piece *Politics*, essayist Ralph Waldo Emerson likened the railroad to mankind's more artistic forms of expression:

We must trust infinitely to the beneficent necessity which shines through all laws. Human nature expresses itself in them as characteristically as in statues, or songs, or railroads.

Not too many years later, commenting on the transcontinental railroad, Emerson continued his romance with the

Charles Dickens

railroad, echoing the sentiment of people everywhere:

> And the Iron Horse, the earth-shaker, the fire-breather
> . . . shall build an empire and an epic.

The once pastoral landscape of America, quiet and undisturbed, was now pierced by the sight and sound of a mechanical marvel, the locomotive and its trailing cars. For some it was magical excitement that promised fairy-tale adventure. To others it was a shattering of an old and good social order, and the creation of a new and uncertain world.

Wherever tracks were hammered down, business was sure to follow. Sometimes whole towns were planned around a railroad track, with the track set down alongside the main street. Buildings that had once been inns and taverns catering to the stagecoach trade became rail depots.

A new social caste system was spreading in the wake of the railroad. Now there was a "right side" and a "wrong side" of the tracks.

The right and wrong side of the tracks was determined by which way the wind blew the sooty, black engine smoke. Wherever the prevailing winds and air currents took that smoke became the "wrong side." The wrong side was the cheap rent side, the side of factories and mills, the side of the poor and the debtor. No one wanted to work or live on the wrong side of the tracks if he or she could help it. The right side, on the other hand, became the side of the expensive shops, churches, the finest homes, and the wealthy.

Right side or wrong side, by 1852 there were 9,000 miles of railroad track in America. England had only about 6,500 miles of track. Most of the American track lay in the Northeast, some in the South. But like a giant iron web, the rails linked up and spread ever westward. By 1854 a traveler could board a train in New York, arrive in Chicago, board the Chicago & Rock Island Railroad, and travel to Rock Island on the east bank of the Mississippi River—the end of the line at the time. If the traveler had business further west, he had to first take a boat to Davenport, Iowa, on the opposite bank and then mount either a horse or take a stagecoach to wherever he was going.

Meanwhile, the builder-owners of the Chicago & Rock Island Railroad, Henry Farnam and his partner, Thomas C. Durant, had surveyors plotting a new railroad, the Mississippi & Missouri. These tracks would stretch 298 miles across Iowa from Davenport to Council Bluffs, a frontier town on the Missouri River. Farnam & Durant had further plans to bring their tracks to Omaha, Nebraska, a ramshackle town on the other side of the Missouri River. They envisioned laying their tracks all the way to the Pacific Coast, if they could. It was one thing, however, to bring the iron

preceding page:
The Lackawanna Valley, an oil painting by George Inness, 1855.
Beyond the approaching train on the left side of the tracks is a town near Scranton, Pennsylvania. On the right side is the new roundhouse of the Delaware, Lackawanna & Western Railroad. The painting was created as an advertisement. It shows how the railroad changed the American landscape.

NATIONAL GALLERY OF ART

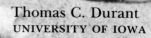

Thomas C. Durant
UNIVERSITY OF IOWA

Henry Farnam

horse to a river's edge. It was another thing to get the railroad across the river. There were no bridges spanning the Mississippi or the Missouri, let alone a bridge engineered to accept the load and strain of a locomotive pulling a set of cars.

Farnam & Durant formed the Railroad Bridge Company. They pressed hard to obtain the necessary government permits to build a connecting railroad bridge across the Mississippi River. Time and again riverboat men complained about the idea. They claimed that the bridge would be an obstruction to navigation. Businessmen from one end of the Mississippi to the other, whose commercial well-being was tied to the north-south river traffic, viewed the east-west crossing of the railroad as a threat to their establishments. They sensed that the expansion of the railroad farther west would destroy the chances that any one of the great Mississippi River cities would become the commercial and cultural center of the nation. Urged by southern steamboat owners, southern politicians in Washington tried to prevent the bridge's construction.

None of the protests prevented Farnam & Durant from constructing the 1,535-foot wooden Rock Island Railroad Bridge. On April 22, 1856, the first passenger train to cross the Mississippi River rolled across the bridge into Davenport, Iowa.

"Swiftly we sped along the iron track," a reporter wrote. "We're over. . . . We have crossed the Mississippi in a railroad car." Back East a Philadelphia newspaper told its readers, "Civilization has got safely over the Mississippi by steam."

Two weeks later, the sidewheeling steamboat *Effie Afton* slammed into the bridge and blew up, destroying part of the bridge as well. The owners of the vessel sued the builders of the bridge, Farnam & Durant. They claimed that the

A view of the Mississippi River, 1860s. The railroad bridge from Rock Island to Davenport can be seen in the far right distance.
PUTNAM MUSEUM

bridge was a hazard to navigation. Farnam & Durant retained Abraham Lincoln, a reputable 47-year-old lawyer. Lincoln argued that the boat was crippled before it hit the bridge, that it had collided with a structure that could not move out of the way, and that the boat was to blame for the collision and not the bridge. Some railroad people hinted that the whole thing was staged so that the courts would have a reason to prevent the building of more railroad bridges across the Mississippi, but nothing ever came of that.

Lincoln made it very clear to the rest of the country that railroads had every right to travel east, west, north, or south; that boats had that same right; that neither had the right, however, to interfere with the continuous transit of the other; that rails were to a train what water was to a boat; and that if a bridge was necessary to take a train over a river, then that bridge had a perfect right to be there. Lincoln won his case.

The suit received nationwide attention. The decision was upheld by the Supreme Court. The case brought Lincoln and his homespun courtroom style to the attention of powerful Illinois Republican politicians on the lookout for a presidential candidate. Two years later Lincoln was elected sixteenth president of the United States. When Lincoln came to Washington in 1861 to take the oath of office, he entered the nation's capital by train, on the Baltimore & Ohio—the B & O.

Abraham Lincoln, 1857
LIBRARY OF CONGRESS

4.

The Civil War

By the time the Civil War started in 1861—a war fought between a progressive industrial North and a conservative agricultural South—there were at least 200 operating railroads in America. The largest group of these ran in, around, and out of the Northeast. The second-largest congestion of rail lines was in the Midwest in a great ellipse formed by Chicago, St. Louis, Cincinnati, and Cleveland. There were a few lines in the South, and there was nothing but stagecoach service and the pony mail express in the Far West.

As the Civil War raged on and bloodied the country, the railroads became a necessity of military life—and open targets. The North, with its vast network of tracks, used the rail lines to ship troops and supplies to the battle areas. The Baltimore & Ohio, being the closest rail line to some of the major Virginia battlefields, was subjected to constant harassment by Confederate raiders and southern sympathizers. B & O tracks were regularly ripped up along with other equipment. Timbered trestle bridges over steep valleys, a favorite target, were burned, repaired, and burned again. The B & O built an armored rail car and mounted a cannon up front to fight off the raiders.

One of the chief targets of southern sympathizers in Virginia was the B & O railroad bridge where the Shenandoah

Harper's Ferry, photographed by Alexander Gardner, 1865
VAN PELT LIBRARY, UNIVERSITY OF PENNSYLVANIA

48

and Potomac rivers meet at Harpers Ferry. It connected Maryland with western Virginia. "This bridge has been so often destroyed during the last five years," wrote Alexander Gardner, a Civil War photographer, "that it is estimated that a million of dollars have been spent in keeping it in repair."

It was at Harpers Ferry that an act of armed violence against the government of the United States sent a chill through the country as it lurched toward civil war.

An eastbound B & O train carrying U.S. mail had stopped at the Harpers Ferry station in the early morning darkness of October 17, 1859. As it prepared to leave the station and cross the bridge into Maryland, John Brown and 18 of his followers, fanatical abolitionists whose hatred of slavery had already led to wanton murder in Kansas, stopped the train. Kansas had been torn by fighting between those like John Brown, who wanted to put an end to slavery, and southern

sympathizers, who pledged themselves to preserve it. Now John Brown and his supporters were in the East—in Virginia—and had invaded government property—the U.S. arsenal at Harpers Ferry. In addition, they had captured the B & O railroad bridge across the Potomac River.

Brown, a large, bearded man, instructed the conductor of the train, A. J. Phelps, and the engineer, William McKay, to contact the Secretary of War, John B. Floyd, to tell him that no further trains would be permitted through; that all communications in and out of Harpers Ferry would be cut just as soon as they let this train go, and that his army of 1,500 men was about to free the slaves in the South. The train was then released, but not before John Brown and his band fired on the crew, killing Mr. Hayward, a black porter, ironically the very symbol of all those slaves John Brown was determined to free.

John Brown had taken possession of the B & O bridge and the arsenal the day before. No one knew exactly what he was up to. Some say he took the arsenal for its weapons, which he intended to use in his planned invasion of the South. Others thought his purpose was to create a fortress at Harpers Ferry in which he could house and protect freed slaves. Whatever his purpose, John Brown was now responsible for three crimes at Harpers Ferry in addition to those he had committed elsewhere: the forcible takeover of U.S. government property, interfering with the U.S. mail, and murder.

The following day marines under the command of an army colonel, Robert E. Lee—the very same Lee who would lead Confederate armies against the federal government during the coming war—stormed the arsenal and captured Brown. Brown was tried for treason and convicted. He was hanged on December 2, 1859.

In February 1861, seven southern states seceded from the Union and formed their own country, the Confederate

John Brown, 1859

States of America. They were Alabama, Florida, Georgia, Louisiana, Mississippi, South Carolina, and Texas. Jefferson Davis, a graduate of West Point and former secretary of war under President Franklin Pierce, became president of the Confederacy. Richmond, Virginia, became the capitol.

On Washington's birthday, February 22, 1861, president-elect Abraham Lincoln, on his way to Washington for his inaugural, left his B & O train briefly to make a speech at Independence Hall, Philadelphia. Faced with the awful prospect of civil war and a divided country, Lincoln told the throng: "If this country cannot be saved . . . I would rather be assassinated on the spot than surrender it."

On April 12, 1861, Confederate troops bombarded Fort Sumter, a federal installation in the harbor of Charleston, South Carolina. The fort surrendered two days later. On April 15, President Abraham Lincoln responded by issuing a call-up for 75,000 troops. Arkansas, North Carolina, Tennessee, and Virginia declared the call-up an act of war and joined the Confederacy. The western counties of Virginia refused to go along with secession from the United States. Instead those counties seceded from Virginia and called themselves West Virginia, becoming the 35th state in the Union two years later. The Civil War had begun, a war whose outcome would largely depend on the railroad.

Photographer Alexander Gardner described the war's opening action in Virginia:

> One of the first operations of the war (upon the Potomac) was the destruction of the wharf and depot of the Fredericksburg and Richmond Railroad at Aquia Creek, done by a small flotilla under the command of Capt. Ward, U.S.N., whose flag-ship was a N.Y. towboat, turned into a gunboat, and called the Freeborn. The buildings were fired by shells, the enemy kept up a lively fire also. . . . The rebels gave up the blockade of the Potomac. . . . The wharf was rebuilt, . . . enlarged and improved . . . a town of hastily but well-constructed buildings . . . among them, and close upon the railroad tracks, the Provost Marshal's Office.

Railroads came under increasing attack by both sides as the war spread west. Railroads, never before used as such, became war machines. Flatcars were used to haul heavy mortars into firing positions. Other cars towed high-flying observation balloons, used mostly by federal troops to spot Confederate positions. The trains delivered the troops, arms, and provisions for battle, as well as removing whole armies from war zones.

In March 1862, a Confederate army retreated from the Manassas-Centreville battleground in Virginia toward Rich-

Railroad ruins at Manassas Junction, photographed by Alexander Gardner, 1862
VAN PELT LIBRARY, UNIVERSITY OF PENNSYLVANIA

mond aboard trains of the Orange and Alexandria Railroad. As the troops left they made sure that the Union troops would not follow them. They set fire to the railroad's depot, idle railroad cars, locomotives, wagons, repair and machine shops, warehouses, surrounding buildings, and fortifications at Manassas Junction. They also destroyed the bridge south of Manassas Junction by fire to prevent Union pursuit. The destruction was complete. The Confederates got away. Manassas Junction was left a smoldering, desolate level plain.

Both sides, North and South, did everything possible to destroy each other's ability to move men and equipment. Thus the railroad with its depots, junctions, and miles of track became a prime target. One line, the Louisville & Nashville Railway, which operated about 270 miles of track in western Kentucky and Tennessee, was hit more often than any other railroad. The L & N tried to maintain a neutral position in the war. One end of the line was in Tennessee, which had seceded from the Union. The other end was in Kentucky. Kentucky, a slave state, took no side. Half of the population had sided with the Union; half with the Confederacy. Kentucky declared itself neutral.

When Tennessee seceded, the governor of Tennessee, Isham Harris, seized that part of the railroad in his state. The Union banned all goods leaving Kentucky for Tennessee, hoping to starve the state into submission. Southern sympathizers in Kentucky nevertheless managed to send carload after carload of provisions into Tennessee on the L & N.

Confederate troops tried to keep the Union—its men, guns, ammunition, and supplies—off the L & N in Kentucky. Confederate general Simon Bolivar Buckner attacked the line. He was stopped some 40 miles south of Louisville, the railroad's Kentucky terminus. Union general

Damaged Rails
NATIONAL ARCHIVES

Train derailment at Manassas, photographed by Mathew B. Brady, 1864

William Tecumseh Sherman took back a few miles of the
L & N. Much of it remained in southern hands, however,
until February 15, 1862, when the Union army entered
Nashville, the southern terminus of the railroad. But what
the federal forces found there was not a working railroad
but a wrecked railroad from Nashville all the way to Bowl-
ing Green, Kentucky. The southern forces had already destroyed locomotives and cars. Tracks, too, had been torn
up, hurled into huge fires, and bent or melted down. The
ties were reduced to ashes. The Confederate forces had also
burned bridges, warehouses, and stations and cut telegraph
wires. They destroyed all equipment necessary for the running of the railroad.

The Union repaired the L & N railroad and had it in
fairly good working order by April 1862, when Confederate general John H. Morgan and his band of guerrillas
attacked the line at various sites and tore it apart again. As

quickly as the Union repaired the damage, Morgan's Raiders struck again. They kept on striking the line, sometimes with as many as 4,000 whooping and hollering cavalrymen. Confederate generals Nathan Bedford Forrest and Braxton Bragg did their share to disrupt Union L & N supply lines both in Tennessee and Kentucky. And the Union continued to repair the line through July 1863 as battles were fought to reduce Confederate strength in western Kentucky and Tennessee.

Morgan was captured in Ohio, escaped, and was later killed in Tennessee. Bragg was defeated at Chattanooga by General Ulysses S. Grant, November 23–25, 1863, and at Missionary Ridge by General George H. Thomas, the "Rock of Chicamauga." All of Georgia and Alabama—the heart of the Confederacy—lay before the Union armies. The L & N finally was left in relative peace. The line's locomotives chugged up and down the rails from Nashville to Louisville, safe, but armed to the teeth and protected by a string of temporary forts built along the route.

The Union, too, did its best to destroy Confederate railroads. In April 1862, having just finished repairing the L & N in Tennessee and Kentucky, the Union struck an important supply railroad behind the southern lines.

A Kentuckian Union spy named James J. Andrews and 21 men, all dressed in civilian clothes, casually boarded a Western & Atlantic passenger train at Marietta, Georgia. They told the suspicious conductor, W. A. Fuller, that they were on their way to Chattanooga to enlist in the Confederate army. The train, on its way from Atlanta to Chattanooga, was being pulled by the *General*, a powerful steam locomotive. It halted a few miles past Marietta to permit the passengers to disembark at the Big Shanty Hotel for breakfast.

While crew and passengers were busy eating breakfast,

Andrews and his men quickly uncoupled the *General* and several boxcars. They immediately took off, cutting telegraph lines and tearing up tracks behind them.

Fuller and several men chased the *General* on hastily repaired rails. First they drove in a small car that they took turns powering by a hand lever. Then they followed in several different locomotives on clear tracks that the fleeing Andrews had no time to tear up. All Andrews managed to do was temporarily slow down his pursuers by dumping railroad ties onto the tracks. The chase continued for 90 miles, until the *General* ran out of firewood. Andrews and his men jumped from the helplessly rolling engine. They were captured by Fuller and a contingent of Confederate soldiers in nearby woods. Andrews was hanged along with seven of his men. Six of the raiders were exchanged for Confederate prisoners. The remaining eight were imprisoned in Atlanta but later escaped.

Two of the South's most important rail centers, Richmond, Virginia, and Atlanta, Georgia, were devastated by both Confederate and Union troops, who made sure that not a single locomotive could pull a single car in or out of the smoking ruins.

On June 20, 1864, Grant attacked Petersburg, a railroad center 23 miles south of Richmond. The city was held by strong forces under the command of Confederate general Robert E. Lee. Grant's idea was to destroy Richmond's chief supply line—the railroad—and force the southern troops to either surrender their capital or fight and lose it. The attack turned into a siege that lasted until April 2, 1865. During those nine months, a variety of murderous battles were fought all through the area. Finally, Grant was able to seize the Petersburg rail yards. The southern forces retreated from the city, leaving Richmond helpless.

In July 1864, Sherman reached the outskirts of Atlanta,

General Ulysses S. Grant, photographed by Mathew B. Brady, 1864

despite the fact that he had just been defeated by Confederate general Joseph E. Johnston at Kennesaw Mountain. But the victorious Johnston was inexplicably replaced by General John B. Hood, who attacked Sherman but could not halt Sherman's advance on Atlanta. While Hood entrenched himself inside Atlanta, Sherman seized the city's only railroad—the Western & Atlantic—to cut off Hood's supply lines. Hood retreated from Atlanta, destroying the rail yard and leaving a wrecked city. Sherman marched in on September 1, 1864.

Hood, however, made it difficult for Sherman to maintain his line of communications with Chattanooga by raiding and tearing up the railroad between Chattanooga and Atlanta. Instead of chasing Hood, Sherman let others battle it out with the Confederate general, who was finally whipped at Nashville on December 16, 1864, forcing his retreat all the way to Mississippi. The beaten, bitter men in

Union soldiers tearing up rails in Atlanta, 1864
LIBRARY OF CONGRESS

gray sang:

> "You may talk about your Beauregard
> And sing of General Lee,
> But the gallant Hood of Texas
> Played hell in Tennessee."

A month earlier, on November 15, 1864, Sherman burned Atlanta and began his march through Georgia. The last train out of Atlanta that day was pulled by the *General*. Sherman's army destroyed everything in its path, especially the railroads. Sherman's men ripped up the rails, tossed them into great bonfires, and then took the red-hot rails and wrapped them around trees, calling them "Sherman's neckties" or "hairpins."

Sherman reached Savannah, Georgia, on December 21, 1864, and wrote that his march through Georgia would not

The last train out of Atlanta, 1864. The engine seen at the far left is the *General*. The photographer was George N. Bernard.

have been successful "without the railroads." He promptly wheeled northward into South and North Carolina in an attempt to link up with the Union forces in Virginia.

With federal forces advancing on Richmond, Confederate president Jefferson Davis ordered the city's evacuation. He also ordered Generals Richard Stoddert Ewell and John C. Breckenridge, former vice president of the United States in the administration of President James Buchanan, to burn all war supplies. This included munitions, rail yards, locomotives and cars, and anything that might be of use to the Union troops. They practically burned Richmond to the ground.

Davis fled the city south by rail across the James River via the Richmond & Petersburg railroad bridge on Sunday night, April 2, 1865. The two-deck wood bridge was built on 16 stone piers, with the top deck carrying the railroad and the bottom deck, carriages. On Monday morning, following Davis's flight, the Confederates set the bridge and Richmond on fire. On the Richmond side of the bridge were a paper mill and one of the largest arsenals in the South, all of which were destroyed in the huge blaze. Nearby was the Tredegar Iron Works, which produced most of the Confederate cannons. Somehow it escaped destruction and fell intact into Union hands.

By the war's end, Union forces were repairing damaged rail lines almost as fast as Southern troops could destroy them. The entire railroad repair and rebuilding operation was under the command of General Herman Haupt. A former construction engineer and superintendent of the Pennsylvania Railroad, he was now chief of the Bureau of Military Railroads. General Daniel C. McCallum, former superintendent of the Erie Railroad, president of the McCallum Bridge Company, and Haupt's immediate superior, was in charge of all military rail transportation for the Union.

McCallum, a railroad bridge expert, was appointed to the job by Lincoln's secretary of war, Edwin McMasters Stanton. Stanton made McCallum the undisputed boss of every railroad in the United States, although most of McCallum's attention was focused on the Virginia, Tennessee, and Georgia war zones. He had extraordinary powers not only to keep the railroads running on behalf of the military establishment but to seize any railroad he needed for any military purpose without prior permission. Captured railroads, too, fell under his jurisdiction. McCallum also dictated how the more than 1,000 locomotives and cars were to operate on the 20,000 miles of track under his command.

Originally commissioned a colonel, McCallum received his brigadier general's star when he efficiently used the railroads to shuttle 23,000 troops into Tennessee to ensure Confederate general Bragg's defeat at Chattanooga in the fall of 1863. Earlier, during the 1862 campaign in which Richmond nearly fell, McCallum had his locomotives and cars delivered by ship from Baltimore to the Richmond & York River Railroad in Virginia. The Union army arrived on his trains to within four miles of Richmond. McCallum eventually became a major general. It was his organizational skills that kept Sherman's rapidly moving advance through Georgia just as rapidly supplied by rail.

Herman Haupt, a West Point graduate, was also appointed by Stanton and commissioned a colonel. He, too, would become a general. Haupt seemed to be everywhere at once repairing and rebuilding lines and bridges almost as soon as they were destroyed. When Southern forces burned the Richmond, Fredericksburg & Potomac Railway's wood trestle bridge over the Potomac River, Haupt rebuilt it in a couple of weeks. President Lincoln was so impressed with reports of Haupt's 400-foot-long, 100-foot-high bridge, he

preceding page:
Work crew repairing damaged rails on the Orange and Alexandria Railroad, 1863. General Herman Haupt is the standing figure in the upper right corner. The engine in the photograph was named for him.

went to see it for himself.

"That man Haupt," marveled Lincoln, "has built a bridge across the Potomac Creek . . . over which loaded trains are running every hour, and . . . there is nothing in it but bean-poles and cornstalks."

The South with its 9,000 miles of track, ill-equipped mechanically, poorly organized industrially, and lacking the technical expertise seeded in the manufacturing climate of the North could not repair its damaged railroads in time to ward off the enemy. The North's 20,000 miles of track and its knowledge of building, running, and maintaining oper-

General Haupt's bridge across the Potomac
NATIONAL ARCHIVES

able and serviceable rail lines was a contributing factor to the South's defeat.

The final days of the Civil War and its immediate aftermath were played out on railroads. Early on the morning of April 8, 1865, a train carrying food provisions for General Robert E. Lee's starving army arrived at a station on the Lynchburg-Petersburg rail line three miles from the Appomattox courthouse in Virginia. It would be there that Lee would surrender his 27,000 exhausted troops to General Ulysses S. Grant. As the detail unloaded the train, Union cavalry, under the command of Major General George Armstrong Custer, stormed their ranks.

Photographer Alexander Gardner described the event:

> The supplies were being transferred to wagons . . . by a detail of about four thousand men, many of them unarmed, when suddenly our cavalry charged upon them. . . . The rebel officers made strenuous efforts to force their men to resist the attack, but after a few shots, they fled in confusion.

This was Lee's final effort to feed his hungry men. He failed. His surrender the next day, April 9, ended any hope of a Southern victory. The war was over.

Six days later, on Saturday, April 15, 1865, President Abraham Lincoln died of a single shot to the head. The fatal wound had been delivered by John Wilkes Booth at Ford's Theatre in Washington, D.C., the night before, Good Friday. Booth, a famous actor, murdered the president to avenge the defeat of the South.

A week later, Friday morning, April 21, at eight o'clock sharp, Lincoln's body was placed in a special B & O funeral train. It was then slowly borne in a light rain from the B & O railroad station in Washington to Lincoln's home in

General Robert E. Lee at his home in Richmond, Virginia, photographed in 1865 by Mathew B. Brady.
LIBRARY OF CONGRESS

Springfield, Illinois. Black soldiers lined the station.

The train proceeded at hardly more than 20 miles an hour to Baltimore, Harrisburg, Philadelphia, New York, Albany, Buffalo, Columbus, Indianapolis, and Chicago. Large state funeral processions were held before the train ended the journey in Springfield. The train halted briefly along the carefully planned 1,700-mile route to allow people from countless towns and villages to pay their final tribute. It was the largest outpouring of grief America had ever known.

The funeral train consisted of 10 cars and two highly polished black iron and brass steam locomotives. One of the engines traveled alone and at a distance in front of the train to clear the tracks of any accidents or incidents. The locomotive itself—there would be 12 of them used along the way—was draped with black crepe. American flags, a flower wreath encircling the front of the boiler, and a photograph of Lincoln completed the ornamentation. The first eight cars contained 300 government dignitaries and Lincoln family members. Next came the black-draped funeral car carrying an honor guard along with the bodies of Lincoln

Lincoln funeral train parked on a temporary Lake Michigan trestle outside of Chicago, 1865
CHICAGO HISTORICAL SOCIETY

and his son Willie, who had died earlier. He was to be reburied with his father. A baggage car brought up the rear.

On noon, Wednesday, April 26, the Lincoln funeral train waited at Albany, New York, as six white horses pulled a black hearse containing Lincoln's remains in a city procession. That night John Wilkes Booth was shot and killed in a burning tobacco barn in Virginia. Four of his eight co-conspirators were hanged on broiling, sunny July 7, 1865. The others were imprisoned. Booth had written this in his diary while being hunted down:

> I can never repent it, though we hated to kill. Our country owed all her troubles to him, and God simply made me the instrument of his punishment. . . . I have too great a soul to die like a criminal. . . . Let me die bravely. . . . I have never hated or wronged anyone.

Abraham Lincoln was finally buried in Springfield's Oak Ridge cemetery on May 4, 1865.

5.

The First Transcontinental Railroad

In May 1869, the 37 sovereign states that constituted the United States of America were at peace with one another. Even so, the country was still divided. Although no longer politically and militarily fractured into North and South by civil war, America was now split East and West—geographically, economically, and developmentally.

The populous East, especially the industrial Northeast, undamaged by war and still aglow with victory, was crisscrossed by a fast-growing network of railroads. None of these railroads had been there 40 years before. Most of them appeared in the 1850s and 1860s. These lines carried passengers and freight westward to the banks of the Missouri River—to Council Bluffs, Iowa—a distance of about 1,200 miles from the Atlantic shoreline. Council Bluffs was the end of the line—the very edge of mechanized civilization. On the other side of the river was Omaha, Nebraska. Kansas City and St. Joseph, both end-of-the-line rail depots farther south in Missouri, were not as far west as Council Bluffs, falling short by only a few miles.

Boston, New York, Philadelphia, Baltimore, and Washington, D.C., were linked by rail to the burgeoning midwest cities of Chicago, St. Louis, Kansas City, St. Joseph, and of course, Council Bluffs. All these lines fed into one another in a continuous web of iron and wood. Among the north-

Railroad map of the northeastern United States, 1856
LIBRARY OF CONGRESS

71

east lines of the day were those four major railways that in time would control all the others to the edge of the Mississippi River: the Baltimore & Ohio, America's oldest continuing railroad; the New York Central; the Erie; and the Pennsylvania.

In the Midwest and along the Great Lakes were all those lines that by 1895 would be incorporated into the systems controlled by the B & O, the New York Central, the Erie, and the Pennsylvania. Among these were the Michigan Central; the Michigan Southern; the Central Ohio; the Marietta & Cincinnati; the Pittsburgh, Fort Wayne & Chicago; the Ohio & Mississippi; and the Terre Haute & Indianapolis.

There were scattered rail lines in the South as well, connecting the coastal cities of Wilmington, Charleston, and Savannah with such inland metropolises as Richmond, Memphis, Atlanta, and Chattanooga.

Between the Council Bluffs–Omaha area and the roaring surf of the Pacific Ocean lay the sparsely populated, undeveloped West. There stood soaring mountains with icy, snow-packed passes; endless plains and prairies; wind-whipped canyons; wild rivers; timeless meandering streams; and withering desert heat. There, too, roamed the countless herd of bison, cattle, and wild horses; gunslinging robbers; nervous Indians; and hard-driving cattlemen. In addition, glittering in the light of recent discovery, were California gold and Nevada silver. Beyond and to the north were Oregon furs and Washington lumber. In all that vastness—several million square miles—there was not a single railroad open for public business.

Travelers to the Pacific Coast and places in between detrained at Council Bluffs, after they'd taken the Chicago, Rock Island & Pacific out of Chicago. There they crossed the Missouri River to Omaha on flatboats. They continued west by ox-drawn wagon, stagecoach, horseback, muleback, keelboat, river raft, or on foot.

Mormons traveling west in covered wagons
LIBRARY OF CONGRESS

Whatever the mode of travel, going west beyond Omaha could take weeks or months, should a traveler remain alive. He had to survive the scorching heat of the plains in summer and the bone-cracking mountain cold in winter. He had to survive snowstorms that often killed a traveler in 30- and 40-foot drifts. He had to outrun those angry Indians who viewed his presence as an invasion of their lands. He had to survive the crushing stampedes of thousands of buffalo, whose pounding, thundering hooves, lost in clouds of dust, could be heard for miles. He had to survive robbers who took everything he had and left him with nothing more than the clothes he wore—and his life, if he was lucky.

As early as 1832, Hartwell Carver, a doctor in Rochester, New York, wrote a series of articles proposing that a transcontinental railroad be built from Lake Michigan to Oregon.

John Plumbe, a onetime railroad surveyor who practiced law in the Iowa Territory, was another individual with an early plan for a transcontinental railroad. In 1838, he drew up a petition for a railroad that would link the West Coast with eastern railroad lines. He sent the plan to the Congress in Washington, D.C., and was promptly ridiculed for his vision. Plumbe left Iowa for Washington. He pursued his railroad dream to a dead end and became a photographer.

In 1840, he established the first chain of photography studios in the world when he opened the Plumbe National Daguerrian Gallery and Photograph Depot in Washington. Photography was only a year old. His studios extended all the way from New York, Boston, New Orleans, and Louisville to Paris, France. He took the first photographs of the city and some of the nation's best-known people at the time. President Andrew Jackson and Sam Houston had their first photographic portraits taken by Plumbe.

Plumbe went broke, however, and took off for the California goldfields to remake his fortune. Failing to find any gold, he spent months surveying land and seeking backers for his transcontinental railroad. Unable to finance his idea, he gave up, defeated by those in the East and Midwest who brought their railroad schemes to life. Crushed and despondent, John Plumbe returned to Iowa in 1857 and committed suicide.

Another dreamer of transcontinental railroads was Asa Whitney, a New England shipping merchant who specialized in trade with China. He thought a railroad across the country would make the journey faster than a long sea voyage from the east around South America and across the Pacific to China. He promoted his idea of a nationwide railroad for seven years, from 1845 to 1852. Whitney's line would take a northerly route that would originate on the shores of Lake Michigan and end at Puget Sound on the Pacific. He badgered every congressman, senator, and government official. His plan would be to buy 78 million acres from the government for a few cents an acre, push the Indians—Native Americans—off their ancestral lands, if necessary, and get on with the laying of tracks.

In 1848, friends of his in the U.S. Senate actually introduced a bill to sell Whitney so-called public lands at 16 cents an acre to construct his railroad. It mattered little that the lands would be ancestral homes of Indian tribes. The bill was defeated by Senator William Hart Benton of Missouri, who wanted a transcontinental line to start from St. Louis. Whitney retired to his farm near Washington, D.C., but the dream of a cross-country railroad remained. Plainly, more powerful interests than Whitney's, determined to build a railroad across the country to suit themselves, got him out of the way.

James Gadsden, U.S. minister to Mexico, wanted a transcontinental railroad to take a more southerly route to the Pacific through El Paso, Texas. The federal government obliged him by buying 45,535 square miles of land in New Mexico and Arizona from Mexico for $10 million. The treaty, called the Gadsden Purchase, was signed on December 30, 1853. It extended American boundaries farther south and made it possible to put a southerly routed railroad on American soil. The Civil War interfered with the project, however, and it came to nothing.

The wheels to ease transportation across the country coast to coast were set in motion in 1861 by Theodore Dehone Judah, an intense young civil engineer from Connecticut. Judah was a graduate of Rensselaer Institute. He had railroad experience. He had worked for the New Haven, Hartford & Springfield and Connecticut Valley railroads. He had designed and constructed the Niagara Gorge Railroad. Judah came to California in 1854 to build a 21-mile railway for a mine operator. The railway was completed the following year, in 1855. It stretched from Sacramento to the gold mines near Folsom in the foothills of Sierra Nevada. But Judah had another vision. He dreamed and talked endlessly of a transcontinental railroad. And he knew what he was talking about.

Following the completion of the mine railway, Judah began to survey the mountainous terrain of Sierra Nevada for a company that wanted to build a wagon road from Sacramento to the Nevada silver mines. He had little use for the wagon road and insisted that rails should be constructed through the mountains instead. The wagon road company was not interested, but Judah continued to investigate. He and a friend, Dan "Doc" Strong, a Dutch Flat pharmacist, located an ideal rail route through the mountains along the

from left to right: Leland Stanford, Collis P. Huntington, Mark Hopkins, Charles Crocker

Truckee River. Returning from the survey, Judah stopped at Doc Strong's Dutch Flat drugstore and wrote "The Articles of Association of the Central Pacific Railroad of California."

He spoke everywhere, including Washington, D.C., in an effort to drum up interest and money for his transcontinental railroad. He resurveyed the terrain. Eventually he made a proposal to a number of wealthy Sacramento businessmen. He suggested that since silver had recently been discovered in Nevada, they should build a railroad into the Nevada Territory to Virginia City. It would put the silver lodes within their grasp. Among this interested group were four merchant tycoons. They were the "Big Four": Leland Stanford, who would become president of the railroad and governor of California; Collis P. Huntington; Mark Hopkins; and Charles Crocker. These enterprising men had amassed their fortunes selling groceries and hardware to

the swarms of gold-seeking hopefuls who had been invading California since the discovery of gold in 1848. They formed a partnership with Ted Judah, supplying the money to build his railroad to Virginia City.

While the rest of America headed toward civil war, Theodore D. Judah built the railroad from Sacramento through Sierra Nevada to the Nevada mines. But Judah's idea of extending the tracks eastward never left him. He buttonholed politicians and pleaded for the right to continue the Central Pacific's tracks all the way to Omaha. There, at Omaha, the Central Pacific would link up with the Chicago, Rock Island & Pacific line on the other side of the Missouri River and thus give America its first transcontinental rail line.

No one listened to Judah. The operators and owners of the various stagecoach lines especially despised his scheme, as they knew full well that a transcontinental railroad would destroy their passenger and freight business. In an effort to

Theodore Dehone Judah
LEONARD EVERETT FISHER

discredit Judah, they began calling him "Crazy Judah" and "Crazy Ted." Ted Judah never got a chance to see his dream come true. Differences over money and charges of fraud began to dissolve the connection between the partners. In September 1863, the Big Four bought out Judah's share for $100,000, which sent Judah back East to raise more money to buy out the Big Four. In November, while en route, he contracted yellow fever and died.

Since neither Ted Judah, John Plumbe, Asa Whitney, nor anyone else had put a rail line across the country to the Pacific, the co-owners of the Chicago, Rock Island & Pacific, Farnam and Durant, wanted to be the first. Henry Farnam, interestingly enough, knew very little about the extent of his partner's financial wheeling and dealing. Durant had been conniving behind Farnam's back to grab everything for himself—not only the railroads, but the land under the tracks as well. It mattered little who had landed rights beneath his tracks—the Indians; the U.S. government; farmers; ranchers; or anyone else who staked his claim in the open, lawless West. Thomas C. Durant was out to gather in the land for himself at cheap rates, build his railroad, and sell off the excess land at enormous profit.

Unlike his partner, Henry Farnam, who envisioned a transcontinental railroad to serve the interests of the country as well as himself, Durant saw the railroad as a means to line his pockets with money. He despised Henry Farnam for his vision, his work ethic, and his honesty.

Like the Mississippi & Missouri, the Chicago & Northwestern was laying track across Iowa aimed at Council Bluffs. Durant, a member of C & N's board of directors, successfully schemed to take over the C & N. He then schemed to dissolve the firm of Farnam & Durant, got rid of Henry Farnam, and remained in sole control of the Mississippi & Missouri and the Chicago, Rock Island & Pacific, the only rail routes from Chicago, Illinois, to Omaha, Nebraska. Thomas Durant, now the principal owner of the Chicago, Rock Island & Pacific, had chosen Council Bluffs as a terminus for the line with the idea of eventually extending it across the Missouri River. By the time Lincoln was inaugurated, the Chicago & Rock Island Railroad had merged with a rival rail line, the Chicago & Northwestern, changing its name to the Chicago, Rock Island & Pacific. The addition of "Pacific" had been Farnam & Durant's signal that they were planning to shape their railroad into a transcontinental line. They were not alone in their transcontinental ambition.

Even before "Crazy Judah" had caught the transcontinental rail fever, Durant had persuaded the Omaha Indians to sell him their ancestral lands on the western side of the Missouri opposite Council Bluffs. He called the ramshackle town Omaha, after its former owners. From there he had planned to lay 1,500 miles of track to San Francisco. Omaha had become the perilous outpost of one man's ambition and one country's destiny—"the manifest destiny of the people to move westward," said Abraham Lincoln.

On July 1, 1862, President Lincoln signed into law the Pacific Railroad Act, resolving the issue of a transcontinental railroad and the route it would take. Lincoln and his generals were uneasy over the possibility that the Confederacy, with whom they were at war, could launch a strong attack on the Union from California with help from western sympathizers. With a transcontinental railroad, Northern troops could be moved West quickly to meet the challenge. The idea had been discussed for years. Every time it came before Congress, Southern representatives and senators blocked it. They were not against a transcontinental railroad; rather, they were opposed to such a railroad having a northern route. They wanted a southern route. With the outbreak of the Civil War, however, Southern legislators left the Congress, thus leaving no obstacle to the creation of the railroad across the north.

Under the terms of the Pacific Railroad Act, two lines were awarded construction contracts: the Central Pacific, which had not yet laid a single track, and the Union Pacific, the name of the new line that would lay track westward from Omaha. Money for the project would come from government loans, from the sale of land freely granted to the railroads by the government, from a $16,000 government bonus for every mile of track laid, and from the sale of stock to private investors.

Thomas Durant became one of the first board members of the Union Pacific. In 1863, Durant and several other senior members of the board connived to form a company called Crédit Mobilier. Crédit Mobilier was owned by the stockholders of the Union Pacific. Its purpose was to let out construction and supply-purchase contracts for the railroad. The terms and prices of these contracts were thus determined by the very men who were directors of the Union Pacific. In effect, Crédit Mobilier had control of the Union Pacific's money, and the several officers had unlimited powers over the management of the railroad. The stockholders could become rich and the major stockholders richer.

The scheme was simple enough. Since Crédit Mobilier was in charge of spending the Union Pacific's money, the directors of Crédit Mobilier were able to tap into the railroad's funds by overcharging the railroad for work or for supplies and then pocketing the money that was left over. For example, if a shovel cost $1, Crédit Mobilier would bill the railroad $2. Since Crédit Mobilier was in charge of the transaction, it paid the supplier of the shovel the $1 received from the railroad and kept the additional $1 for itself.

The same thing applied to construction. For example, if the building of a toolshed cost the railroad $1,000, Crédit Mobilier would bill the railroad $2,000. Again, since Crédit Mobilier was in charge of the transaction, it paid $1,000 for the construction and kept the additional $1,000 for itself. Durant and others also received an extra 10 percent in kickbacks from almost every construction contract they let out. That is to say, when a contractor received $1,000 for building a toolshed, he subtracted $100 of that amount and gave it back to Durant and his cronies, who simply pocketed the money.

In addition, the directors of Crédit Mobilier made money by selling off land bordering the railroad. Since they had never had to pay for the land in the first place—the land had been granted to the Union Pacific by the government—the stockholders were able to realize huge profits.

None of the monies belonged to Crédit Mobilier, to Durant, or to the Crédit Mobilier stockholders. It all belonged to the Union Pacific. Yet the excess money from work and supply contracts that found its way into the Crédit Mobilier bank account ended up in the pockets of the Crédit Mobilier stockholders as dividends, including the $16,000-per-mile bonuses. And since Thomas Durant and his close friends were the major stockholders, most of the money ended up in their own private bank accounts. Although Durant was not the president of the Union Pacific (General John A. Dix was president), he controlled the railroad as chief stockholder of Crédit Mobilier.

By 1868, Durant and his friends had paid themselves such enormous dividends that Crédit Mobilier had sunk about $6 million into debt and could not pay the rail workers their meager salaries. Durant was kidnapped by track workers and imprisoned in his private railcar until he made arrangements to pay the considerable wages due the workers.

Durant lost control of the Union Pacific in 1872 to a scheming Massachusetts congressman, Oakes Ames, and his brother, Oliver. The brothers had become rich by manufacturing shovels, an important tool in railroad construction. In 1865, shortly before he was assassinated, President Abraham Lincoln appointed Oakes Ames to the board of the Union Pacific to straighten out the tangled financial affairs of the railroad and to improve the slow track-laying schedule. Almost immediately, the Ames brothers began to purchase stock in Crédit Mobilier. By 1872, they had become the major stockholders in Crédit Mobilier and forced Durant out. Oliver Ames replaced General Dix as president of the Union Pacific. The Ames brothers milked the company of so many millions of dollars, perhaps as much as $23

Oakes Ames

million, that Crédit Mobilier went further into debt. The government was finally prompted to investigate.

The inquiry revealed, among other corruptions, that Representative Oakes Ames had given key congressmen stock in Crédit Mobilier. Oakes Ames had positioned himself to control congressional votes on any matter that would concern the Union Pacific. Ames had committed an unethical act, if not an actual crime—bribery. And he admitted it, saying that he gave out the stock "where it would do the most good." Worse still, he voted on a company in which his brother was president and in which he was a major stockholder—a conflict of interest, if not illegal. Ames was impeached. He was disgraced by a vote of Congress, but never prosecuted. He soon died of a stroke. Durant was never called upon to account for his earlier corrupt wheelings and dealings.

Finally, in 1863, work began at both ends of the proposed transcontinental line—at Sacramento and at Omaha. One year later, in 1864, and despite unimaginable difficulties (equipment had to be brought by sea to California from New York by way of the southern tip of South America), the Central Pacific offered the public a 31-mile service between Sacramento and Newcastle, in the Sierra Nevada foothills. The run took anywhere from one hour and fifteen minutes to an hour and forty-five minutes, with stops at Junction, Rocklin, and Pino. Omaha, Nebraska, was still 1,500 miles and five days away. By the end of 1866, the Union Pacific had laid 300 miles of track, pushing westward to the North Platte River.

Construction west from Omaha was under the direction of Peter A. Dey, a civil engineer who quickly resigned because he thought the construction contract was dishonest. "I do not care to have my name . . . connected with the railroad," he wrote.

Dey figured the cost of laying the first 100 miles of track to be $25,000. But the Crédit Mobilier directors let out a contract for $50,000, raking in $25,000 as profit for themselves. All the while, as mentioned before, Crédit Mobilier—Durant and his friends—were pocketing $16,000 of Union Pacific money received from the federal government for every mile of rail laid by the sweat of men who earned $2 or $3 a day, untold thousands from stock dividends, and more thousands from the sale of land granted to the railroad by the federal government which had cost them nothing to begin with.

Dey was replaced by Grenville M. Dodge. For 10 years prior to the Civil War, Dodge, a civil engineer from Massachusetts, roamed the Midwest surveying tracts of land for possible railroads. He had also surveyed a possible rail route from Council Bluffs, Iowa, along the Oregon Trail toward Salt Lake. Dodge, who lived in Council Bluffs, rose to the rank of major general during the Civil War in the 4th Iowa Infantry. He was twice wounded and did outstanding service in repairing and reconstructing war-torn railroads.

It took six years to build the transcontinental railroad between Omaha, Nebraska, and Sacramento, California. None of it was easy. Roadbeds had to be carved out of the rugged mountains at dizzy heights and angles. Tunnels had to be blasted through those mountains. Crude wooden, tunnel-like "snowsheds" had to be built to protect tracks, trains, and work crews from gigantic snowslides and drifts. Many a Central Pacific laborer lived in these windy, frigid snowsheds as the difficult work went on. Throughout the continuing struggle men died. They died of disease, of the cold, by accident, from bullets, and from tomahawk wounds.

By the afternoon of Monday, May 10, 1869, the rails finally met at a place called Promontory, a desolate spot on

Snowshed

the northern rim of the Great Salt Lake in the Utah Territory. The connecting point of the Union Pacific and Central Pacific railroads was some 850 miles due west of Omaha and about 650 miles northeast of Sacramento. Omaha, Nebraska, was no longer eastern America's outpost in the West. On May 10, America "East" joined America "West." It took the back-breaking labor of an army of Irish, German, and Scandinavian immigrants, ex-slaves, convicts, and veterans to lay the westbound tracks of the Union Pacific. The tracks of the Central Pacific were laid eastbound through the treacherous snow-clad Sierra Nevada by more Irish immigrants, veterans, a few Indians, and some 15,000 Chinese laborers. The Chinese proved themselves heroic when, in a single day, April 28, 1869, they extended the tracks of the Central Pacific a record-breaking 10 miles.

America now had a railroad that stretched from the Atlantic to the Pacific—a transcontinental railroad. The ceremonies that took place that day at Promontory, in the Utah Territory, marked one of the biggest nationwide celebrations since the British surrendered at Yorktown, Virginia, in 1781, following the final battle of the Revolutionary War.

Leland Stanford, former governor of California, and Thomas Durant stood before a noisy crowd of laborers, drunks, shady ladies, professional gamblers, some dignitaries, a couple of brass bands, and soldiers of the 21st Infantry Regiment. After missing their first strokes, to the jeers of the crowd, the two men finally pounded gold and silver spikes into the last tie. The transcontinental railroad was a national fact of life. A wire attached to one of the spikes was meant to send the sound of the silver-headed sledgehammer striking the spike across the country by telegraph. It did not work. A telegraph operator in Omaha picked up the one-word message from Promontory. "Done" was all that came over the wires. He faked the sound of hammer

April 28, 1869, the day the Central Pacific Railroad laid ten miles of track in 24 hours
SOUTHERN PACIFIC RAILROAD

blows by tapping them out to the rest of the nation himself.

"1869 May 10th 1869 . . . GREAT EVENT," proclaimed the vivid ornate poster. "Rail Road from the Atlantic to the Pacific . . . GRAND OPENING of the UNION PACIFIC . . . avoiding the Dangers of the Sea . . . LUXURIOUS CARS & EATING HOUSES . . . PULLMAN'S PALACE SLEEPING CARS. . . ."

America exploded in a merrymaking din of bell pealing, whistle blowing, cannonading, singing, shrieking, parading, and prancing as the Central Pacific's locomotive No. 119 and the Union Pacific's Jupiter nudged each other. Great crowds in Chicago; Buffalo; Philadelphia; New York; Boston; Washington, D.C.; San Francisco; and Sacramento took to the streets and congratulated each other. America, awash in a sea of pride and patriotism, whiskey and wonder, celebrated her new unity while the happy throng at Promontory climbed all over the facing locomotives and had its picture taken.

Bret Harte, whose stories of the West were popular everywhere in America, commemorated the occasion:

"What was it the Engines said,
Pilots touching—head to head
Facing on the single track,
Half a world behind each back?"

Five days later, May 15, the first transcontinental rail service was opened to the public. The trip took some 10 or 12 days, depending on weather, breakdowns, and other troubles. Fares westbound from Omaha ran between $40 for a hard bench and $100 for a luxurious sleeper. These fares doubled if the journey was full length, New York to California. They did not include meals taken in the undistinguished "eating houses" that lined the tracks westward or

preceding page:
Meeting of the Central Pacific and Union Pacific Railroads at Promontory, Utah, May 10, 1869
LIBRARY OF CONGRESS

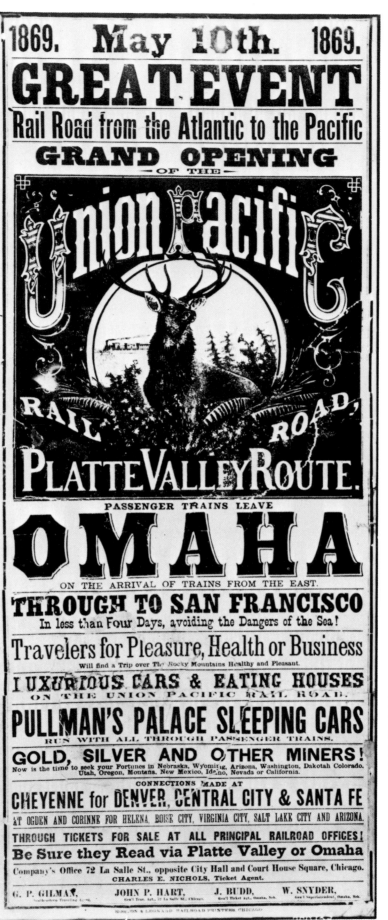

Poster announcing the grand opening of the transcontinental railroad
LIBRARY OF CONGRESS

eastward.

There were no dining cars during the early years of transcontinental rail travel. And not until 1875 did any one traveling across the West have anything but the worst food imaginable. Fred Harvey, a one-time New York dishwasher, St. Louis and New Orleans restaurant owner, and Kansas cattle agent, changed all that. In 1875, he talked the Atchison, Topeka & Santa Fe into allowing him to operate a string of first-class restaurants along the railroad's route. The first of these opened in what used to be an ordinary lunchroom in the Topeka, Kansas, depot. Harvey cleaned it up, painted the place, installed new furniture, added white linen tablecloths and napkins, polished silverware, and provided an excellent cuisine of the freshest and finest foods, served by waiters who were gradually replaced by uniformed waitresses. And with the women came more elegant restaurants, each called Harvey House, and more gracious service.

The waitresses, known as Harvey Girls, were an unheard of addition to the wild and woolly, often desolate Southwest. Table service had been the trade of men. Harvey wanted the women waitresses from the beginning, but the rough western women were not graceful and refined enough for Harvey. He recruited women from the East by newspaper advertisements calling for "Young women of good character, attractive and intelligent, 18 to 30."

Harvey dressed his "girls" in black with white collars, white hair bows, and white aprons. The women lived in dormitories presided over by a motherly matron. They earned $17.50 a month plus tips, room, and board. They had to be in the dormitory by 10 P.M. So many of them married as soon as they arrived on the job that Fred Harvey made them sign a contract giving up half their pay if they married during the first year of employment. By 1900, there were 47 Harvey Houses to accommodate the railroad passengers of the Southwest. The Harvey Girls had become world-famous.

Besides the scheduled half-hour dining stops, trains made other frequent stops crossing the country. They handled freight and mail, took on water, and allowed time for passenger "necessities." These frequent stops, together with an average speed of about 25 miles per hour, gave the passengers an unhurried look at the seemingly endless American landscape. From the windows they could see cowboys and Indians, shaggy buffalo, lowing cattle, and howling coyotes.

Harvey Girls

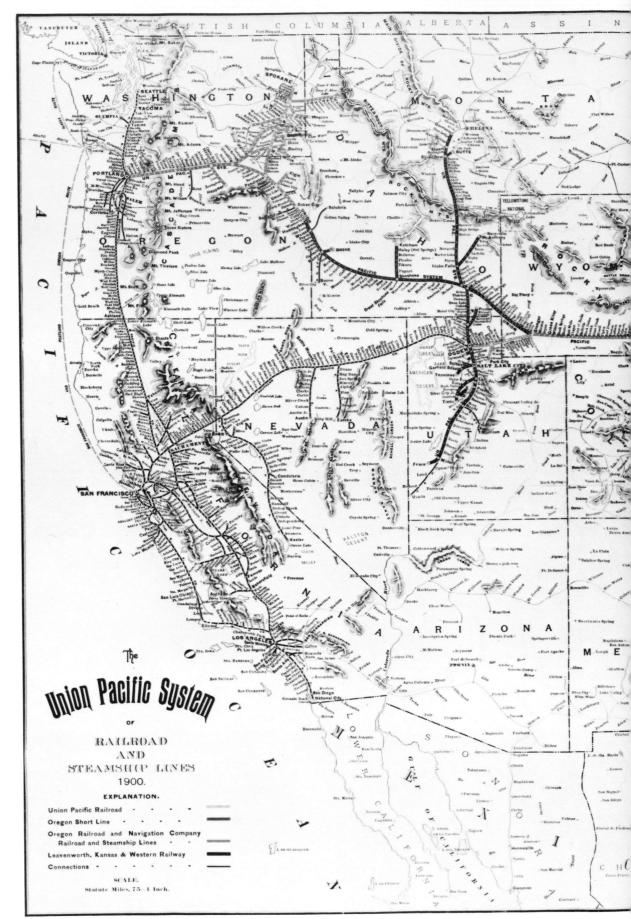

Map of the development of the Union Pacific System, 1869–1900

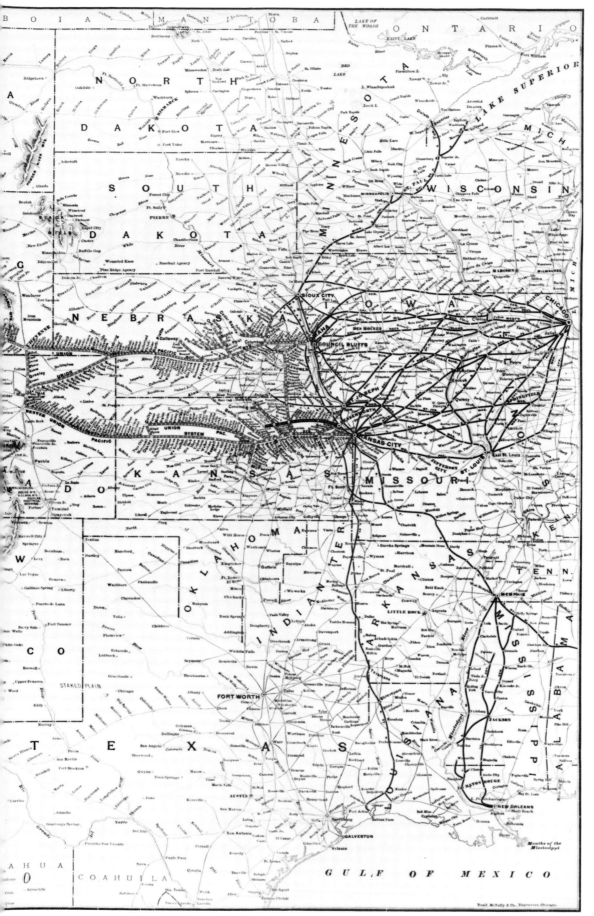

6.

Native American Resistance

About 1 million Indians—Native Americans—lived on the North American continent at the beginning of European colonization in the early 1600s. By 1900, the Native American population had dwindled to about 300,000, reduced by disease, hunger, abuse, betrayal, wars of survival, and the contempt of white European civilization.

The Sioux, Cheyenne, Arapaho, Crow, Blackfeet, Kiowa, Pawnee, and other great Indian nations watched with growing alarm and anger as the 19th-century wagon trains rolled west to spread the white man's civilization over their ancestral hunting grounds.

From time to time they attacked the wagons in an effort to turn back the tide. The U.S. government set up army posts along the Oregon and Santa Fe trails and elsewhere to protect the westward migration. John L. Sullivan, a New York newspaperman, coined the expression "manifest destiny" when he wrote in 1845 that it was "our manifest destiny" to own and govern all of North America. President Abraham Lincoln, as noted in the previous chapter, agreed. Lincoln owned properties in Council Bluffs that he had acquired in payment for a debt and for his military service in the Black Hawk War. That war was fought in 1832 between white settlers and the Sauk and Fox Indians over possession of Rock Island, Illinois, then an Indian village. The Indians lost Rock Island. In a larger sense, these Native Americans were fighting to stop further westward expansion of white civilization.

In 1847, essayist Ralph Waldo Emerson noted in his journal that "the timeless locomotive must be conceded. To us Americans, it seems to have fallen as a political aid. We could not else have held the vast North America together, which now we engage to do." The American nation had to be one nation "from sea to shining sea," as Katherine Lee Bates would say in 1893 in her anthem "America the Beautiful."

Between 1825 and 1860, the railroad spread from the Atlantic shoreline to the Mississippi and across the Missouri into Indian tribal lands. These tribal lands, deeded to the Indians by solemn treaty, looked very promising to the entrepreneurs of Eastern civilization. Therefore, the white man rewrote the treaties he had previously negotiated whenever convenient. The government squeezed Native Americans into even smaller pockets of undesirable land or "reservations."

In California and Nevada, Paiute and Shoshoni tribes, who were hostile to the oncoming Central Pacific, were bought off by Collis Huntington, one of the Big Four, in a remarkable treaty. First, he lived up to a promise to pay them—man and woman alike—to work on the railroad alongside his army of Chinese laborers. Then, as Huntington himself tells it:

> We gave the old chiefs a pass each, good on the passenger cars, and we told our men to let the common Indians ride on the freight cars whenever they saw fit.

The railroad civilization clanked on. More and more, Plains Indians in the path of the Union Pacific's tracks and, later, several northern railroads were unable to cope with

Freight train passing through Umatilla Indian Reservation, Oregon

their changing world. The iron horse was an invasion of land that they had always lived on and an intrusion that they were unwilling to accept.

Trouble started in Minnesota before any tracks were laid. At the outset of the Civil War, the regular soldiers stationed at the scattered outposts in Minnesota that had been set up to protect the wagons rolling west had been transferred to the fighting fronts. They were replaced by inexperienced volunteers who offered little or no protection. Some young Sioux took advantage of that weakness and killed five settlers near New Ulm in August 1862. This was followed by a one-week rampage in which 700 settlers were killed. The Minnesota militia fought the Sioux, led by Chief Little Crow, in a fierce battle. Two thousand Sioux were captured, and Little Crow was killed. Three hundred were tried for murder in St. Paul, and 38 publicly hanged.

The Sioux were so outraged by the calamity that had befallen them at the hands of the white man that for the next 28 years, they battled to keep white civilization out of their territory.

Three years after the New Ulm slaughter, U.S. troops tried to build a road from Cheyenne across Wyoming to newly discovered Montana goldfields. The goldfields were in Sioux and Crow territory at Powder River and Big Horn. Sioux chief Red Cloud and his braves drove the troopers off. Another military expedition was sent with orders to tell Red Cloud that the United States would build the road peacefully or by force, if necessary, and that Red Cloud should consider the consequences if he resisted. White speculators with influence in Washington were after the gold that belonged to the Sioux and Crow nations.

The government called for negotiations it never meant to honor. Red Cloud met at Fort Laramie in the Wyoming Territory with the army commander, Colonel Henry B.

Chief Red Cloud
SMITHSONIAN INSTITUTION

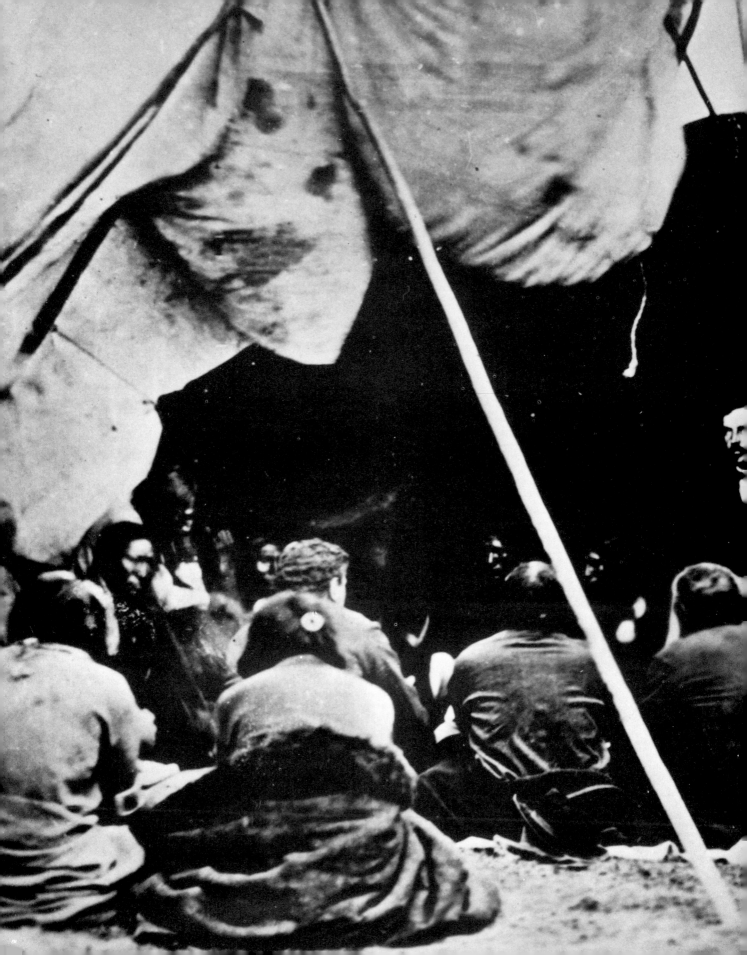

Carrington. Red Cloud listened to U.S. threats delivered by Carrington. "I will talk with you no more. I will go now," Red Cloud replied, "and I will fight you for the last hunting grounds of my people." He stormed out of the meeting.

Colonel Carrington followed his orders to the letter. His own personal views, however, were that the United States had no right being on Indian land to begin with.

"There never was a more ill-considered impulse of the American people," Carrington would later write, "than that which forced the army . . . to serve the behests of irresponsible speculative emigration, regardless of the rights of tribes rightfully in possession."

The Sioux as well as other nations had only to look at what happened to the Cherokee, not a generation before, to know what was in store for them if they did not try to resist the white man's takeover of their ancestral hunting grounds. In 1829, gold was discovered in northern Georgia on land deeded by the U.S. government to the Cherokee nation "in perpetuity." The discovery brought thousands of white prospectors swarming illegally over the region, demanding that the government declare the treaty canceled. President Andrew Jackson responded nine years later by driving every Cherokee off the land by force and cruelly escorting the entire nation all the way to Oklahoma. The forced march, in which many died, was called the Trail of Tears. The white man's word meant little where his greed and ambitions conflicted with Native American rights.

The U.S. government did almost nothing to protect the interests of the Indians. It perceived them as savages who stood in the way of progressive civilization, whose culture was totally alien to American interests. The angry Indians attacked the railroad as it coursed its way west. There were too few federal troops in these areas to protect the railroad builders. For their part, the rail workers were

preceding page:
Treaty meeting at Fort Laramie, Wyoming, photographed by Alexander Gardner, 1868
NATIONAL ARCHIVES

armed and fought back. The Indians carried off many a scalp and gave up their own lives in what they considered a just war for survival.

During the 1870s, promoters of rail travel, railroad owners, railroad building contractors, and land developers were pressuring President Ulysses S. Grant and Congress to get the Indians out of the way. They argued that Native Americans threatened the safety of travelers. Native Americans obstructed the laying of track. Native Americans did not use the land as it was meant to be used—for farming and cattle ranching.

The truth of the matter was that Native Americans lived on land that developers wanted to turn into money. Some of that land was bought cheaply and outright from the Indians. Some of it was just grabbed. Native Americans, these business interests argued, generally blocked the progress of civilization that had been marching westward ever since ancient Greece and Rome. The Civil War, which had divided the nation, disrupted its vision, and fractured its unity, was over. Civilization was on the move again—west! American "manifest destiny" was on the move again—west! The president wanted no further delays in the expansion to the west. The Native Americans—the Indians—had to either move aside or perish.

The fast-growing population in the East and Midwest, thickened by European immigrants, had to have a steady supply of meat, among other staple foods, for their tables. Meat was a bodybuilding food for those who stoked the furnaces of the mills, refineries, and factories on whose steady production the country had become more dependent. America was no longer just a farming community. Large segments of the population used the railroads to leave the farms to work in the mills, refineries, and factories of the cities. Meat had become an essential part of their diet.

Railroads could bring western cattle to the Chicago stockyards and slaughterhouses more cheaply and quickly than any other means of transport. And from Chicago, the butchered and dressed meat would find its way by rail again to the shops, stoves, and dining tables of the American working family.

In the late 1860s, a Kansas meat contractor, supplying a dwindling food ration to the railroad workers, hired a crack-shot, ex-Pony Express rider to shoot some buffalo and replenish the meat supply. He was William F. Cody, soon to be known as Buffalo Bill. Cody was so good and so fast a hunter that he could drop a dozen buffalo with almost as many shots—on the gallop—before a fairly competent hunter could take aim. Nearly single-handedly, Buffalo Bill fed the army of railroad workers with his smoking rifle. It became fashionable to hunt buffalo, even from the windows of moving trains, and few people sensed the

Buffalo skins drying in Dodge City, Kansas

William F. Cody, "Buffalo Bill"

possibility that the buffalo was now an endangered species and could disappear from the American continent.

Even worse, few knew or cared that the starvation of the Plains Indians over the cold winters was directly linked to the killing of the buffalo to feed hungry railroad builders. For generations, Plains Indians had selectively killed buffalo. They used the meat over the winter for food and the skins for clothing. They never threatened the herds, since they only killed as much as they needed. White entrepreneurs, on the other hand, had an insatiable hunger to kill buffalo for food and sport. Not only was buffalo meat used to feed thousands of railroad workers the year round, buffalo hide was sent east to be made into clothing, rugs, and other products like footwear and handbags. The killing went on indiscriminately. If the buffalo were to disappear from the Great Plains, the Indians would have no food supply. That would mean death to their culture, but no one thought much about the future of the Native American.

"A good Injun is a dead Injun" could be heard in every rail town that rose on what once was Indian land. And death was visited upon untold numbers of Indians who would not be pushed onto reservations.

In the 20-year period between 1865 and 1885, an estimated 12 million buffalo were slaughtered. What the hunters did not kill, what the Indians themselves did not kill, the people on the onrushing trains finished off by shooting at the great beasts from train windows.

In contrast, Dr. Brewster Higley's popular verse written in 1873 expressed a romantic vision of the West:

> "Oh, give me a home where the buffalo roam,
> Where the deer and the antelope play,
> Where seldom is heard a discouraging word
> And the skies are not cloudy all day."

The Buffalo Hunt, an oil painting by Frederick Remington, 1890
BUFFALO BILL HISTORICAL CENTER

By the 1880s, there were four other transcontinental railroads chugging across the West in addition to the Central Pacific–Union Pacific lines: the Atchison, Topeka & Santa Fe; the Northern Pacific; the Great Northern; and the Southern Pacific. The building of all these lines met strong challenges from Sioux, Crow, Blackfeet, Arapaho, and Cheyenne, among others. But it was the Sioux opposition to white settlement and the laying of Northern Pacific tracks in the Dakota and Montana territories that provided one of the most celebrated defeats in U.S. military history—the annihilation of George Armstrong Custer.

During the 1870s, Indian attacks on western settlers and railroad builders had become more frequent. Eastern and now midwestern business interests were growing impatient with territorial settlement. There were vast quantities of rich raw materials to be brought out of the West by the railroad. Lumber, minerals, ore, and grain, meat, and other foodstuffs were becoming more essential to the economy of the rapidly growing nation, which was moving swiftly toward full industrialization.

President Grant reacted to the pressure of business interests and the nation's eagerness to have complete control of all its territories from the Atlantic to the Pacific. He wanted to ensure completion of the railroads to accomplish this, so he called in the army. He ordered General Alfred H. Terry to squeeze the troublesome Sioux and Cheyenne onto confining reservations. No further obstacles to the building of the Northern Pacific Railroad, the Kansas Pacific, or the Union Pacific would be tolerated. Included in the military expedition was the U.S. Army's crack 650-man Seventh Cavalry Regiment, commanded by a noted vain and pompous Civil War hero, Lieutenant Colonel George Armstrong Custer.

George Custer was often referred to by his rivals as the Boy General or Glory Seeker, since he was a 21-year-old general during the Civil War. He was known as Long Hair to the Indians, who despised him. He was despised by the men under his command as well, after he ordered soldiers caught going AWOL—absent without leave—summarily shot without investigation or trial.

Indian hatred of Custer stemmed from his fierce attacks on the Sioux, Arapaho, and Cheyenne encampments in western Kansas and Oklahoma. Indian attacks on the railroad track men had become more intense and violent. One telegraph repairman, William Thompson, was scalped alive.

General George Armstrong Custer, photographed
Mathew B. Brady during the Civil War

"It just felt as if the whole head had been taken off," he reported. Thompson found his scalp and lived to tell the tale.

Custer had originally been sent to Fort Dodge in western Kansas to drive away and finally kill off the Indians who were then trying to stop the westward advance of the Kansas Pacific Railroad. His orders from General William Tecumseh Sherman were to "destroy their villages and ponies; to kill or hang all warriors and bring back all women and children." Custer went on a rampage. He and his cavalry wantonly killed Indian men, women, and children in western Kansas and leveled their villages.

Earlier, in 1864, Black Kettle, chief of the southern Cheyenne, signed a treaty of peace with the government and brought his tribe to live at Sand Creek in eastern Colorado. He even raised an American flag over his tent to indicate his loyalty to the United States. On November 29, 1864, troops

under the command of Colonel J. M. Chivington stormed the unarmed Sand Creek settlement at dawn and slaughtered the sleeping Indians. The entire country was appalled by the betrayal and the murderous, unprovoked attack. Black Kettle's wife died in the assault. He survived to sign two more treaties with the government, which allowed him, and what remained of his people, to live in peace.

The second of these arrangements was the 1867 Treaty of Medicine Lodge. The treaty placed Black Kettle and his people on a desolate reservation. In return, Black Kettle was promised supplies and arms to hunt buffalo, which the government failed to hand over. Black Kettle and his people slowly starved. When Black Kettle turned up at Fort Larned, Kansas, in July 1868 to ask for the promised arms and supplies he had never received, he was turned away.

"We hope the Great White Father will take pity on us," Black Kettle pleaded, "and let us have the guns and ammunition he promised us so we can go hunt buffalo to keep our families from going hungry."

The government relented and turned over the promised weapons and supplies. Black Kettle hunted buffalo and settled in western Oklahoma on the Washita River. On November 27, 1868, in the mist of a snow-covered winter dawn, George Armstrong Custer and his Seventh Cavalry, which included Osage Indian scouts, slashed through Black Kettle's village, killing him and nearly everyone else. The southern Cheyenne were never again a force in anyone's way. But other Indian nations, in particular their allies, the Arapaho and Kiowa, the northern Cheyenne, and the Sioux, would never again trust a white man's document or promise. They waged war against the railroad more furiously than ever before while their hatred for George Armstrong Custer smoldered for eight years.

On Sunday, June 25, 1876, ten days before the United

The only known photograph of Chief Black Kettle (seated second from left in bottom row)
OKLAHOMA HISTORICAL SOCIETY

States would celebrate its 100th birthday, Custer, riding into the Montana Territory on General Terry's orders, sighted an Indian encampment reported earlier by army scouts. Seemingly small, it was quietly nestled in the valley of the Little Big Horn River. Estimating that he was outnumbered only a little less than two to one—perhaps a thousand Indians to his 650 troopers—and seeking the advantage of surprise, Custer quickly divided his regiment into three columns. He sent the first column under Captain Frederick W. Benteen to the hills on his left to protect his flank. He sent Major Marcus A. Reno with the second column charging directly into the camp. He himself led the third column of some 225 men into the hills on his right, aimed at attacking the encampment from the side.

But there, in those hills to his right, Custer met his doom with stunning finality. Five thousand Indians, meeting in a great war council called by Sioux chief Sitting Bull, rose up out of the Little Big Horn and wiped out the column to the last man. The fight "did not last long enough to light a pipe," according to Indian veterans of the massacre.

For the Sioux chief, Sitting Bull, his lieutenant, Chief Crazy Horse, and others, the battle, commonly known as Custer's Last Stand, was the most momentous victory ever won against the white man. But the results of the Battle of the Little Big Horn, which were not known for some 10 days, proved to be without strategic merit in the Indian war against the railroad. The white man went on pursuing the red man with more vigor, overwhelming him with the iron horse.

It was not only the army, the Indian fighters, and the powerful westward pressure of the eastern population that weakened the Indian will to resist. Hunger, disease, and disillusionment also sapped the Native American fighting spirit and allowed the railroad to creep across the plains as it spread the white man's culture from east to west, from ocean to ocean.

7.

Rivals and Robbers

The fighting and killing along the railroad tracks were not confined to white men versus red men and buffaloes. The railroad workers fought among themselves in bitter rivalry, too.

Most of the men who labored to build the railroads were young and tough. Many were unmarried. Some were semi-skilled and unskilled American-born laborers. Others came straight from Europe, where recruiters working for the railroads convinced them that they would be better off laying track in America than remaining poor and impoverished in Ireland, or Italy, or Germany, or wherever they were from. The Chinese, who came mostly from southern Chinese provinces, knew that to remain in China meant certain unemployment, poverty, and starvation. It took little to convince them to cross the Pacific Ocean and work on the railroad.

Resentment of one group of workers toward another group was constant. Most of the time resentment flared over having to compete for jobs. When white workers, blacks, Chinese, and even Native Americans were not competing for work, they fought one another over racial differences.

Irish rail workers on the Central Pacific in California, Nevada, and Utah rioted against the railroad's hiring of competing Chinese laborers. Not only did the men fight

one another along the tracks, but they battled in the towns. In addition, there was occasional infighting. Irish rivals from Tipperary and Cork, Ireland, fought each other for employment on the Erie Railroad in New York. They sang about the mayhem when their grueling work day was done:

> "In eighteen hundred and forty-six,
> The gang pelted me with stones and bricks,
> Oh, I was in a hell of a fix,
> While workin' on the railway."

Pitched battles were not uncommon in the seedy little wood-and-canvas towns that sprang up at the edge of the newly laid tracks. Hard and dangerous work by day spilled into the crowded, rowdy saloons at night. There, a river of whiskey, too few dancing girls, restless cowboys too long on the range, and any number of trigger-happy drunks could spark a murderous melee, and often did. Even as the tracks of the Union Pacific and Central Pacific approached and then deliberately passed each other while more track got laid at government expense, the rival work crews broke from their back-breaking labors and fought one another in wild brawls. With the government paying the railroads $16,000 bonuses for every mile of track laid, neither the Central Pacific nor the Union Pacific wanted to meet the other at Promontory. As the tracks passed within sight of each other, the work gangs quit what they were doing and fought just to keep one or the other from advancing too far.

Sometimes the fighting verged on warfare between railroad lines. In 1879, the Atchison, Topeka & Santa Fe Railroad hired William "Bat" Masterson to prevent a rival line, the Denver & Rio Grande, from laying tracks southward

Anti-Chinese riot in California
CULVER PICTURES

117

across Colorado into New Mexico. The Santa Fe line intended to keep for itself the old Santa Fe Trail route through the Raton Pass on the Colorado–New Mexico border. The trail, a nearly 800-mile-long stretch between Independence, Missouri, and Santa Fe, New Mexico, was one of the oldest and longest trade routes in America before the coming of the railroad.

Masterson, former sheriff of Dodge City, a notorious and unruly Kansas cow town on the Santa Fe line, took his sharpshooting dentist friend "Doc" Holliday and 29 other gunmen to Canon City, Colorado. There a gun battle broke out between Masterson and his group and a similar army of mercenaries hired by the Denver & Rio Grande Railroad. No one was seriously hurt. But Masterson and his friends won the day. The Denver & Rio Grande owners thought twice about a southerly route into New Mexico. Instead, they went westward into Utah. The Atchison, Topeka & Santa Fe not only went south through Raton Pass into New Mexico, but turned westward, rattling across Arizona to southern California.

Not all rivalries set men against men. Some rivalries set man—John Henry—against machine, or so the story goes. In 1870, John Henry, a black steel driller, was working on the Big Bend Tunnel in West Virginia for the Chesapeake & Ohio Railroad. A bet was made that Henry could pound holes in rock deeper and faster than the new steam drills. Henry made the holes by pounding a steel drill with a 10-pound, long-handled hammer. The holes were then packed with explosives, which were detonated to clear a rock formation.

Even though Henry succeeded in pounding holes deep into the rock more quickly than the steam drill using a 30-pound hammer, he died as a result of his effort. His feat

Atchison, Topeka & Santa Fe Railroad riflemen
at Royal Gorge, Canon City, Colorado, 1879

was immortalized in a ballad known to every worker on the rails:

> "John Henry got a thirty-pound hammer,
> Beside the steam drill he did stand.
> He beat that steam drill three inches down,
> An' died with his hammer in his hand,
> Lawd, Lawd!
> Died with his hammer in his hand."

Besides the workers and lines that were competing with one another, there were those who saw the railroad as a means to gain wealth for themselves. There were fraudulent characters who sold railroad stock for railroads that did not exist or sold stock for the control of a railroad and pocketed the money for themselves. There were land grabbers who used their power and influence to obtain land under or near the rails for nothing or next to nothing and then sold it for enormous sums. And there were robbers who obeyed no law but their own and who eyed everything a train carried—gold, silver, payrolls, mail, freight, passenger possessions—as fair game.

From that day in May 1869 when the transcontinental became an American fact of life at Promontory, few rail lines escaped brutalization by train robbers. This was especially true in the West and Far West, where long stretches of unguarded, isolated railway invited attack.

The Reno gang—four brothers and their friends—was among the first to make a habit of holding up trains. In 1866 the men began a life of railroad crime in southeastern Indiana. The gang relieved an Ohio & Mississippi Railway baggage car of a safe containing about $15,000. After a few more robberies, a murder, and nearly $150,000 in their packs, the men were caught. They were locked up on a train and sent to Seymour, Indiana, to stand trial. They never arrived. A band of angry horsemen stopped the train, yanked off the gang, and hanged the men from trees that lined the tracks.

The most famous of all the western desperadoes were the James brothers, Frank and Jesse, born and raised on a Missouri farm. They fought in the Civil War on the side of the Confederacy as guerrillas hitting the enemy with surprise raids. Almost as soon as the war ended in 1865, the James "boys," a gang that included other surly characters like Cole, Bob, John, and Jim Younger and Robert Ford, continued their forays against small, helpless banks. They were never caught.

On July 21, 1873, the James boys and their friends turned to railroads. That night they tore up a track at Adair, Iowa—about 35 miles east of Omaha, Nebraska—and toppled the locomotive of the Chicago, Rock Island & Pacific, crushing the engineer to death. They held up the train, taking $4,000 in cash and jewelry from the passengers, and then escaped. Between the holdup and 1881, when a price was put on Jesse's head and the remaining Younger brothers were captured, Frank and Jesse and a few new hands terrorized western banks, stagecoaches, and railroads at will. They killed and robbed as they went.

The railroads hired private detectives—"Pinkertons"—to find, arrest, and break up the James gang. The Pinkertons worked for Allan Pinkerton, who established the country's first detective agency. Pinkerton protected Abraham Lincoln on the Baltimore & Ohio as the president-elect journeyed to Washington to take the oath of office. Also, he organized the federal Secret Service during the Civil War. After the war Pinkerton men were used chiefly in the service of railroads to hunt down and apprehend train robbers and to break up mobs of striking workers for railroads and other corporations.

The public often did not support the Pinkertons. People

felt more victimized by greedy railroad companies than by train robbers. They were outraged by the high prices railroad companies were charging for the sale of public land that had been given to them at little or no charge by the federal government.

The people began to think of train robbers as avenging heroes. Railroads were the villains, not hard-riding bandits whose derring-do was regularly romanticized in dime novels everywhere. During the 1870s in California, for example, the Southern Pacific Railroad received land grants from the federal government along each side of its tracks. The railroad passed through the San Joaquin Valley between San Francisco and Los Angeles, one of the most fertile growing areas in the world. By 1880 the railroad was promising to sell these lands to farmers settling by the railroad for $2.50 an acre, as soon as it received clear title. The farmers were willing to buy at that price. But when the title was cleared, the price soared from $2.50 to $10 and then to $30 an acre. The farmers of the Kings' County Mussel Slough area south of Fresno went to court to dispute the railroad's right to the land. They lost. In May 1880, the railroad began to evict those farmers who refused to pay the stated prices per acre. A mass meeting was held. United States marshals and railroad men confronted the farmers at the meeting to remove them from "railroad property." One of the railroad men opened fire on the meeting. A battle broke out. Five farmers and two federal marshals were killed. Accused of murder, 17 farmers were sent to prison. Such episodes encouraged the public to think of outlaws like the James brothers as heroes.

It became increasingly difficult for the Pinkertons to find and apprehend robbers and murderers like Frank and Jesse James. Those who actually knew of their whereabouts—including some lawmen—remained silent. Finally, in April

Jesse James
LIBRARY OF CONGRESS

1882, while living under the assumed last name of Howard in St. Joseph, Missouri, the James gang came to the end of its thieving, murderous career. Jesse was shot in the back of the head by his erstwhile partner in crime, Robert Ford. Ford betrayed Jesse to collect the $5,000 reward put on his head by the governor of Missouri. And the rest of the country sang:

> "Jesse leaves a widow to mourn all her life,
> The children he left will pray
> For the thief and the coward
> Who shot Mr. Howard
> And laid Jesse James in his grave."

Another gang that rode against railroads and banks, leaving a trail of robberies and murders in its wake, were the Dalton brothers—Grattan, Emmett, William, and Robert. Between 1890 and 1892, the Daltons regularly raided the Southern Pacific and somehow always escaped the railroad posses that chased them. Three of the Daltons—Grattan, Emmett, and Bob—and some allies met their end in Coffeyville, Kansas, when they tried but failed to rob Coffeyville's First National Bank and Condon Bank at the same time. Every citizen who could handle a firearm was waiting for them behind windows, doors, trees, bushes, wagons, and fences in downtown Coffeyville. In the blazing gun battle that followed, all of the robbers were shot dead, as were four Coffeyville men.

In no time at all railroad officials, sensitive to the gold, silver, and payroll shipments aboard their trains, became more alarmed over the thieving bent of American bandits than they had been over the murderous attacks by marauding Indians. The robber was interested only in snatching money and not in wrecking the railroad, although a wreck

Robbers on the railroads
NEW YORK PUBLIC LIBRARY

124

or two in the interest of a well-planned robbery was never ruled out.

The first robbery on the transcontinental line took place on November 5, 1870. An eastbound Central Pacific train out of Sacramento, California, was carrying passengers and a $40,000 payroll for the miners of Virginia City, Nevada. Some robbers stopped it on the California-Nevada border in the dead of night and removed the entire payroll. On the night of November 6, 1870, the same train was stopped again. This time it was on the Nevada-Utah border, some 350 miles from where it had been halted only 24 hours before. Again it was robbed of still another sum of money, by a different gang.

Travel back and forth on the western leg of the transcontinental railway was nothing less than a life-and-death struggle. Those who dared to take the trip challenged the elements; the efficiency of the engine that hauled them to wherever it was they were going; the sullen, terrifying Indians; the villainous drifters who plagued the various stops; the wild railroad workers "out on the town" with a week's pay in their pockets, giving passengers good cause to lock themselves up in their cars and draw the shades; and last but not least, those masked desperadoes who derailed and shot up trains to rob them and their passengers of as much of their worldly goods as could be carried off. Hardly a train left a depot without an armed guard in the baggage car and armed passengers sitting nervously in their seats.

Whatever it was that compelled Americans to travel the country by train—business, adventure, a new life, new experiences, sightseeing, or the hair-raising exploits they read about in those countless dime novels—they boarded the trains by the thousands. With bags and baggage, they moved by rail in every direction—north, east, south, and west, but mostly west.

8.

The Owners

Following the war, and during the brief period from 1865 to 1870, financially powerful railroad interests in Baltimore, Philadelphia, and New York resumed expanding their enterprises, an activity that had begun in the 1850s. Now the aim of these interests was to invest in other rail lines beyond their immediate grasp with an eye toward ownership, and to compete with one another for control of others' railroads.

Among those who managed to consolidate and expand the eastern railroad establishment, despite the hazards of stock manipulation, financial frauds, conniving, and court battles, were John W. Garrett of the Baltimore & Ohio; Erastus Corning and Cornelius Vanderbilt of the New York Central; Daniel Drew, Jay Gould, and Jim Fisk of the Erie; and Thomas A. Scott, George B. Roberts, and J. Edgar Thomson of the Pennsylvania. In the west was James J. Hill of the Great Northern.

Garrett became president of the Baltimore & Ohio Railroad not long after the Panic of 1857. The financial panic followed the November 1856 election of James Buchanan as 15th president of the United States. Slavery, the overriding national issue that divided North and South, threatened to tear the Union apart. The country was in a depressed mood' as it headed toward civil war. Woodrow

Wilson, a Princeton University professor who would become America's 28th president, explained the panic 44 years later:

Widespread financial distress clouded the winter that followed the presidential election, and filled all the year 1857 with its deep disquietude, . . . a dull lethargy in which merchants and manufacturers and transportation companies and bankers merely waited and did not hope. The sudden growth of enterprise and commerce which had followed the rapid extension of railways . . . and steam navigation upon the seas, to which the discovery of gold in California had given added stimulation . . . had inevitably bred mere speculation, tempted men to unsound ventures, added excitement to confidence, harebrained scheming to the sober making of plans, and credit had at last been overstrained and wrecked by dishonesty, miscalculation, and flat failure.

The nation's railroads had suffered heavy financial losses during the Panic of 1857. Garrett borrowed money and issued new stock. He immediately reduced expenses. The money he borrowed showed up as earnings. He also showed as earnings monies received from stock that was to be used for improvements. He maneuvered to show that the railroad had earned a surplus of money, convincing investors that the railroad was financially sound and that he was a miracle worker.

Confident investors poured money into the railroad, which Garrett now used to expand the B & O's rails in every direction. The B & O acquired steamboats, docks, hotels, a telegraph company, and grain elevators. Despite the havoc raised on the B & O's rails by the Civil War, Garrett continued to expand the line westward. The railroad earned little money but according to Garrett's magical bookkeeping continued to show great profits while paying generous dividends.

Following the war, Garrett pushed his line farther west and by arrangement began using the tracks of the Pennsylvania Railroad. In 1874, the competition for western business between the B & O and the "Pennsy" erupted into a heated commercial war in which the Pennsy refused to allow the B & O to use its tracks. Garrett responded by cutting his passenger fares and freight rates. Soon all the other lines had to cut fares and rates just to stay in business. What earnings the B & O had managed to scrape up came to a standstill. Garrett borrowed more money and continued to pay a hefty dividend out of the borrowed money. No one had any idea that the B & O was actually broke.

Garrett's son, Robert, took over the B & O's management on the death of his father in 1884. He continued the same policy of expanding the railroad and paying out enormous dividends to stockholders on borrowed money while earning nothing and falling further into debt. By 1896, the bankrupt B & O was in the hands of the courts. The Garrett family no longer had a controlling interest. The railroad was reorganized. New directors were named. New management was appointed. Dividends were halted. The steamboats, docks, hotels, telegraph company, and grain elevators were sold. New multimillionaire investors, like New York banker J. P. Morgan, poured fresh money into the B & O. By the end of the century the B & O was financially healthy.

In 1853, nine small, independent railroads in New York State were purchased by a group led by Erastus Corning, an Albany nail maker. The nine railroads, comprising 560 miles of rail—Mohawk & Hudson; Utica & Schenectady; Schenectady & Troy; Hudson & Berkshire; Tonawanda, Buffalo & Niagara Falls; Auburn & Syracuse; Rochester &

J.P. Morgan

Syracuse; Syracuse & Attica; and Attica & Buffalo—were merged by Corning and his associates into one of the most important rail systems in the country, the New York Central. Erastus Corning became the line's president. The New York Central had passenger and freight service from Albany to Lake Erie. The formation of the New York Central in upstate New York was a death blow to the Erie Canal system, which had already begun to totter when the railroad first appeared. The canal could no longer compete with the speed and efficiency of the railroad in hauling goods and people between Albany and Lake Erie. By 1859, Corning's railroad was a prosperous business headquartered in Albany. Most of its stockholders were ordinary citizens.

Downstate in New York, "Commodore" Cornelius Vanderbilt, a millionaire steamboat operator, turned his eye to the railroad. By the end of the Civil War, Vanderbilt owned the New York & Harlem and New York & Hudson railroads, which controlled all rail business in and out of New York City. The New York & Harlem connected with the New York Central in Albany. Passengers transferred from one line to the other at the Albany depot.

Daniel Drew, president of the Erie Railroad, a rival of the New York Central, sensed that Vanderbilt was after control of both the New York Central system and the Erie. Drew tried to stop Vanderbilt and failed.

During a January 1867 snowfall, Vanderbilt ordered his New York & Harlem to stop short of the Albany depot. Passengers making connections had to walk two miles in the snow to catch the New York Central. As a result, New York Central's earnings and prestige fell. Its stock values tumbled. When New York Central shares hit rock bottom, Vanderbilt bought the railroad.

Wily, tobacco-chewing "Uncle Dan'l" Drew wanted to re-

Daniel Drew

taliate. An ex-cattle drover, he once let his cows get so thirsty that they gulped tons of water just before being weighed in for sale. Uncle Dan'l sold his cows for a good deal more than if the cows had not been so thirsty. The term "watered stock" had its origins with Uncle Dan'l.

Uncle Dan'l named Jay Gould, a clever stock manipulator and railroad speculator, and James "Jubilee Jim" Fisk, who once peddled pots and pans in New England, as his partners on the Erie Railroad. Knowing that Vanderbilt wanted to either buy the Erie or get rid of it altogether, these two—Gould and Fisk—sent word to Vanderbilt that they would make it possible for him to buy enough stock to get control of the Erie. Vanderbilt began to buy the stock. Vanderbilt's interest in the Erie caused a demand on Erie stock. The stock rose to new highs. Gould and Fisk then began to issue more and more stock—fake stock. The price soared. Vanderbilt learned of the trickery and tried to legally stop them. Drew, Gould, and Fisk escaped the clutches of the law by bribing as many crooked politicians as they could and went on printing and issuing $64 million of worthless stock while looting the company of its money from the stock's sale. The public caught on to the scheme and was outraged. Drew, Gould, and Fisk fled to New Jersey with the Erie's cash. The Erie Railroad seemed to be on its last legs. A judge declared the railroad bankrupt.

Uncle Dan'l tried to cool things off while he cooked up another scheme. He sent word to Vanderbilt that he would allow the bankrupt Erie to be merged with the New York Central and repay Vanderbilt all the money he had bilked from him in return for his own participation as a board member of the merged railroads. While Vanderbilt was busy making up his mind, Jay Gould was in Albany bribing some New York legislators with over $1 million worth of stock to pass a law legalizing the fake stock. They did!

Cornelius Vanderbilt

Jay Gould
UNION PACIFIC RAILROAD

Then Drew tried to double-cross his partners and get rid of them. Instead, Gould and Fisk tossed Drew out and left him penniless. Uncle Dan'l Drew died broke. The courts reorganized the still bankrupt railroad in 1870. Jay Gould was placed in charge. Gould began looting the company of its new cash assets. Finally, in 1872, under the threat of arrest and lawsuits he returned millions of stolen dollars to the company. Jim Fisk was murdered that year in a New York hotel over his attention to Josie Mansfield, a popular entertainer. He was given a funeral fit for an emperor. Gould went west, where he maneuvered himself onto the boards of most of the railroads between the Mississippi and California. He died 20 years later after gaining control of the Western Union Telegraph Company and a New York City elevated railroad. His fortune was estimated at some $70 million.

The Erie struggled along until 1900, when it turned itself

Jim Fisk

135

around under new management and became a strong operation.

While clever men manipulated the eastern railroad establishment, Canadian-born James J. Hill, a violent-tempered, shaggy-headed, one-eyed railroad man, built a railroad empire from St. Paul, Minnesota, to Puget Sound on the Pacific. Then he capped his accomplishments by building a castle for himself in St. Paul.

In 1878, Hill headed a syndicate that took over the ailing and nearly defunct St. Paul & Pacific Railroad. He ran its tracks on Minnesota land grants to the Canadian border, where it joined with the Canadian Pacific and changed its name to the St. Paul, Minneapolis & Manitoba. The region began attracting Scandinavian farmers. Hill promoted immigration by offering some of the Minnesota land grant for $2.50 to $5 an acre. Hill was determined to populate the area to increase the profitability of his railroad. He had his eye on extending his rails across the desolate northern plains, across North Dakota, Montana, Idaho, and Washington, all the way to the west coast.

By 1887, the St. Paul, Minneapolis & Manitoba was at Great Falls, Montana. Its tracks were running parallel and north of the near-bankrupt Northern Pacific. Meanwhile Hill had promoted the acreage along the railroad with cheap rates for everything from the transportation costs to the land cost. Once again he populated the railroad's routes with Scandinavian farmers. Hill made it even more attractive by building grain elevators for them all along his tracks. The Scandinavians worked the land, filled up the grain elevators, and shipped their produce on Hill's rails.

Hill did not need any loans, stock manipulations, or subsidies. He simply demanded that towns grant him a right-of-way through their choice districts. Some did. Some did not. Those that did not soon discovered that Hill's construc-

Jim Hill
MINNESOTA HISTORICAL SOCIETY

tion crews made sure that the town would lose out from not having a railroad pass through it. The workers laid tracks so far away from the town that there could be no convenient money-making passenger depot or freight station. Most towns, therefore, were eager to grant Hill anything he asked for.

In 1893, Hill's railroad, now called the Great Northern, reached Puget Sound. The Northern Pacific had failed. Henry Villard, the builder of the Northern Pacific, had borrowed more money than he could repay. Villard's investors pulled out when they could not understand why Villard laid his tracks through a thousand miles of an uninhabited mountainous wilderness. Hill bought a controlling interest in the Northern Pacific. The bankrupt line had now become part of Hill's transcontinental system.

Back east, between 1870 and 1900, Tom Scott, George Roberts, and Frank Thomas each succeeded to the presidency of the Pennsylvania Railroad. Unlike the corrupt Garretts who ran the B & O, the stockholders who ran the Pennsy were honest and kept it financially sound. Scott, Roberts, and Thomson followed stockholder policies and kept a tight rein on the company's business. There was never any stock manipulation, speculation, conniving, or suspicious bookkeeping connected with the railroad in its period of expansion during the last third of the nineteenth century. The company paid regular dividends on actual earnings, not on borrowed money.

The Pennsy kept buying up and improving small lines in western Pennsylvania, Ohio, and Indiana without going into debt as did the B & O. The expansion and consolidation of the Pennsylvania in these regions put the railroad right in the heart of the developing soft-coal country and the very region where, in 1859, Edwin Drake drilled the first oil well. The Pennsy profited, too, from the fact that its

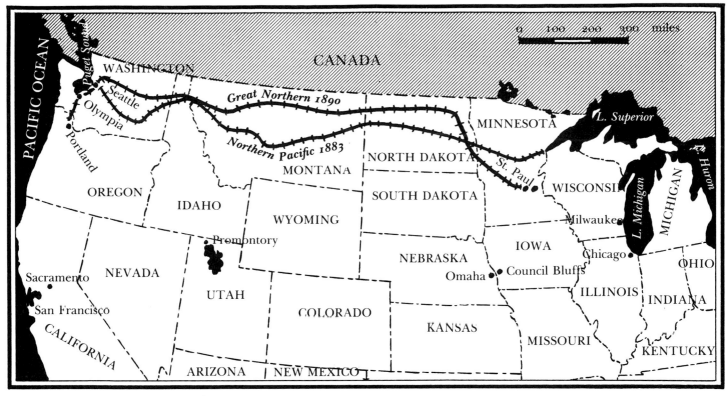

Map of Great Northern and Northern Pacific Railroads
LEONARD EVERETT FISHER

lines led in and out of Pittsburgh, one of the greatest iron, steel, and manufacturing centers in the world. Scott, Roberts, and Thomson not only put company money into rail expansion, they also invested it in their company's freight and passenger service. The high standards of the Pennsylvania Railroad, which reflected the character and ability of its stockholders and officers, made the line the envy of every railroad in the country. There were, however, dark relationships between Pennsy management and the employees of the line. Railroad workers were vastly underpaid everywhere in the country, regardless of the line that employed them. The dollar difference between the poorly paid average employee and the well-paid management was wide and sharp. Railroad workers would not patiently bend their backs forever.

9.

The Car- and Yardmen

Toward the end of the nineteenth century, the business of railroads had put great wealth in the hands of a few people. Such personal wealth and its continuing accumulation caused much unrest and discontent among the railroad workers—conductors, engineers, firemen, brakemen, signalmen, porters, yardmen, construction workers, and the like. They worked for very low wages and endured poor living conditions, while their lives were often at risk.

A. N. Towne, the general superintendent of the Central Pacific, reported this death of a worker in his ledger on February 7, 1878:

> Yesterday a chinaman employed on track attempting to cross the track in front of train No. 7 near Truckee CPRR was run over and instantly killed.

Conductors were the law on the rails. Conductors collected tickets and fares, watched that no one got a free ride, kept the coal stoves in each car red hot during the winter, maintained order, and made sure that everyone got off at his or her proper destination.

Travelers did not always practice good manners. They often would not recognize the conductor's authority, perhaps because conductors were not usually in uniform in the

Conductors on the Michigan Southern and
Northern Indiana Railroads, 1864
SMITHSONIAN INSTITUTION

early years. Conductors experienced difficulty collecting tickets until the end of the Civil War in 1865, when most conductors began to wear uniforms. Brass buttons gave them authority. Some conductors wore pistols, which gave them the additional persuasive force they frequently needed to deal with unruly passengers, assaults by drunkards, and train robbers. Later in the West, conductors added rifles to their personal armament. They tolerated spitting in the aisles of passenger cars but had little patience for whiskey drinkers. Drunks were often unceremoniously tossed off the rear of a moving train. Conductors stood as enforcers of the rules of the railroad and the law in general, and as respected symbols of authority. They represented the company, management, and ownership.

The engineer was the true giant, the legendary hero that most American youngsters yearned to become. He was the driver of the train, the captain of his locomotive, the man

who blew the mournful blasts of the steam whistle as the locomotive rounded a bend or approached a station. The engineer was in charge of his engine and could do almost anything he wanted with it. He decided the sound of the steam whistle, the colors of the engine and its brass fittings, the ornate lettering style of the number and name of the engine. For all this he earned about $4 a day.

Most engineers learned their trade as youngsters doing various jobs around the locomotives in the rail yard. Many of them started as wipers in the roundhouse, greasing the engine's moving parts. The roundhouse was a circular garage with a number of stalls inside for servicing locomotives. Each stall had a track, beneath which was a pit that enabled a mechanic to work under the engine. As many as a dozen locomotives could be serviced at one time. The pay was less than $2 a day.

The wiper climbed the job ladder next as an engine watchman, making sure there was enough steam to move the engine around in the yard.

He then worked as a fireman for about three years, keeping the firebox well fueled and the steam up on the road. But his job did not end with fueling the big locomotives and riding in the cab to the left of the engineer. From time to time, some of the engine's moving parts had to be oiled as the locomotive barreled along at top speed. The fireman had to leave the safety of the cab and walk along running boards against the rushing air while holding on for dear life and squirting oil in and on all the moving machinery. His pay was a little more than $2 a day.

One of the more dangerous jobs in the yard was that of switchman. It was the switchman's job to couple and uncouple trains. The mechanics of doing such a job required the switchman to position himself between stationary cars to

A coupler performing his dangerous job
SMITHSONIAN INSTITUTION

either pull out or insert the pins that linked the cars. At best, many a switchman lost fingers and hands in the link-and-pin coupling process until the introduction of automatic couplers in 1873. Some of the men even lost their lives, when after they had unpinned the coupling, the cars rolled together and crushed them.

The brakeman did not fare any better. The earliest trains were braked by the locomotive. Later, but before the introduction of air brakes in 1869, brakes were manually applied by the brakeman to each car. Usually two brakemen worked a train. They rode on the roof of a fast-moving train exposed to every kind of weather from blistering sun to icy, slippery sleet. There, jumping from car to car, they turned the brake wheels by hand. Many a brakeman died falling off the rocking train or slipping between cars as he strove to leap from one brake wheel to the next.

Central Pacific's general superintendent Towne reported

this accident (#258) on February 19, 1878:

> Today Wm. Lamphrey, brakeman on train No. 7, fell
> off train near Colfax CPRR, severely bruising him.

Chinese immigrants blasted tunnels in the Far West. And
Irish immigrants worked the rails everywhere and at every
job.

The Irish, called Tarriers, fled the famine in Ireland in
1848. They continued arriving by the thousands in New
York, Boston, and Philadelphia for years thereafter. They
formed one of the largest labor pools for heavy American
industries like coal mining and railroading. Some of the
Irish were unskilled pick and shovel laborers. Some were
rock drillers clearing the way for new rails by pounding
holes in rock for the blasting gangs. Their grinding, dangerous work showed up in a popular 1880s ballad:

> "The new foreman was Jean McCann;
> By God, he was a blame mean man.
> Last week a premature blast went off,
> And a mile in the air went big Jim Goff,
> And drill, ye tarriers, drill!
>
> Drill, ye tarriers, drill!
> It's work all day
> For sugar in your tay,
> Down behind of the railway,
> And drill, ye tarriers, drill."

Other workmen filled out the roster of those who moved
the trains from coast to coast, north and south. Depot tele-
graphers let the world know what was happening along the
tracks. Signalmen made sure the trains were running

Northern Pacific workers in Montana,
photographed by F. J. Haynes, 1883

on the right tracks. Porters, most of whom were black, served the passengers traveling on luxurious trains.

The porters, first called "traveling men," were originally ex-slaves hired by the Pullman Palace Car Company in 1867. They were trained in a sleeping car in Chicago. They learned to make beds, store luggage, greet passengers, and otherwise keep luxury train passengers comfortable and happy. After serving a short apprenticeship, they went to work on the rails for $20 a month plus tips. The salary was hardly enough to pay for their uniforms, which the Pullman Company did not supply. Tips were few and far between. The porters pressed management for better wages. Eventually, a half century later, the sleeping car porters would organize themselves into America's first black union, the Brotherhood of Sleeping Car Porters.

There were steel-driving men, track men, graders, and a host of skilled and semiskilled construction workers. Many

of these were Civil War veterans in need of work and adventure and ex-convicts who no one else would hire. Most southern track crews included blacks, as did the transcontinental. Italian immigrants laid many a rail in the East. Hispanics helped to build rail lines in the Southwest. German immigrants filled construction crews in the Midwest.

The majority of workers on the Central Pacific were Chinese. Charlie Crocker, one of the Big Four and now the general superintendent of the Central Pacific, hired nearly every Chinese male in California because he did not have enough workers. Most people who had settled there were able to earn more than what the railroad could pay them and so would not apply for railroad jobs. The Chinese, however, were willing to work for low railroad wages or less.

What started out as a small work force of about 50 Chinese quickly grew to 3,000 and finally to the importation of about 12,000 more from southern China. No job was too mean or too much for the Chinese. Dressed in blue and wearing flat straw hats covering their pigtailed heads, "Crocker's Pets" chopped away at the mountains, often by hand, to make rocky ledges for the tracks. They hauled dirt and rock in wheelbarrows or on their backs up and down the steep terrain. They crawled and climbed or descended to the most difficult places to set their charges and to dynamite tunnels and paths for the tracks of the Central Pacific.

The Chinese workers gambled, noisily argued, and fought amongst each other, but rarely with anyone else unless they were attacked by a white worker, as so often happened. Many a white track worker refused to work with the Chinese and walked off the job. Some of this was due to racial bias. Some of it was due to resentment over the Chinese willingness to work hard and well for little money. The

Dormitory cars like these used by the St. Paul, Minneapolis & Manitoba Railroad in the 1880s housed construction crews.

Chinese workers on the Central Pacific were efficient and reliable and contributed greatly to the building of the Central Pacific from California to Nevada and into Utah. They were considerably less troublesome in the minds of the general public than some of the eastern financial wizards who bankrolled the rails west.

In 1873, Jay Cooke, the financier behind the building of the Northern Pacific, made some disastrous investments as the railroad reached the east bank of the Missouri River opposite Fort Lincoln. The tiny railroad construction encampment at the end of line was named Bismarck, after Otto Von Bismarck, the chancellor of Germany. Cooke hoped to recoup his loss by inducing the Germans to pump money into the Northern Pacific. Unable to get them to do so, Cooke's entire banking empire in Philadelphia collapsed. The Cooke banking failure brought on a panic that led to the ruin of small banks and businesses across the country. Construction on Cooke's railroad line stopped.

The country lost confidence in itself, an enormous depression was under way, and people had little hope for a quick solution. Four million people were out of work, hungry, homeless, and desperate. The people took to the streets.

On a cold January morning in 1874, 50,000 wretched individuals met quietly in Tomkins Square Park, New York City, seeking an answer from government to their plight. As they waited patiently for officials to address them, the throng was charged by mounted police. Many were injured by the charging horses and police clubs. The roaring, frightened crowd fled in every direction, trampling beneath them the wives and children of others. The trouble at Tomkins Square Park was just the beginning.

The depression deepened. Strikes broke out everywhere. On July 16, 1877, the Baltimore & Ohio cut the wages for

Scenes from the Baltimore & Ohio railroad strike, 1877

PENNSYLVANIA.—THE RUINS OF THE ROUND-HOUSE AND PENNSYLVANIA CAR-SHOPS AT PITTSBURGH.

NEW YORK.—RIOTERS TEARING UP RAILS AT THE BRIDGE AT CORNING.

ILLINOIS.—THE FIRST ATTACK BY THE CHICAGO POLICE UPON THE MOB, IN HALSTEAD STREET, ON JULY 26TH.

NEW YORK.—THE CONSTRUCTION GANG REPAIRING THE TRACKS AT CORNING, UNDER PROTECTION OF THE 23D REGIMENT, N. Y. S. N. G.

NEW YORK.—RIOTERS MARCHING DOWN THE NEW YORK CENTRAL RAILROAD TRACK AT WEST ALBANY, JULY 25TH.

NEW YORK.—A MOB THREATENING THE MEMBERS OF THE NINTH REGIMENT, N. Y. S. N. G., AT THE DELAVAN HOUSE, ALBANY, JULY 25TH.

NEW YORK.—THE NINTH REGIMENT, N. Y. S. N. G., TAKING POSSESSION OF THE WEST ALBANY FREIGHT YARDS, JULY 25TH.　　　　NEW YORK.—THE CONSTRUCTION GANG RIGHTING OVERTURNED CARS AT CORNING, UNDER THE PROTECTION OF THE MILITIA.

THE GREAT RAILROAD STRIKE OF JULY, 1877.—SCENES AND INCIDENTS AT THE PRINCIPAL POINTS OF THE LABOR INSURRECTION.—FROM SKETCHES TAKEN ON THE SPOT BY OUR SPECIAL ARTISTS.—SEE PAGE 382.

all its workers. The cuts were so devastating that a working man putting in an eight- to 10-hour day could hardly support himself, let alone his family. Outraged by the cuts, which protected the profits of the millionaire railroad magnates, whose personal lives were not affected by the depression, railroad workers in Martinsburg, West Virginia, seized the line's property. They tied up the railroad's services in and out of the town, offering to restore property and service when their wages were restored. Within days, strikes of railroad workers broke out everywhere. The nation's rail lines came to a halt. Nothing moved between New York and San Francisco.

President Rutherford B. Hayes ordered troops to Martinsburg. The troops were met by the strikers. Shots were fired. Strikers fell dead. Enraged townspeople destroyed the railroad's properties in a pitched battle with the soldiers.

More troops were sent to Pittsburgh, where workers for the Pennsylvania Railroad had struck. The troops were met by other demonstrators. Again shots were fired. Twenty-six people died. Enraged further by the sight of American soldiers shooting at American citizens, more than 20,000 people attacked the 600 soldiers and drove them out of Pittsburgh, destroying much of the city in the process.

Americans in every major city—including New York, Boston, Chicago, Baltimore, St. Louis, and San Francisco—took to the streets to protest the greed of the railroad owners and the use of troops to protect the riches of those owners at the expense of their impoverished employees. Pitched battles between troops, militia, police, and the poverty-stricken, demoralized working people—unemployed for the most part—now occurred everywhere. To many it seemed as if the country was in the midst of an armed rebellion.

Destruction of Pennsylvania railroad equipment
in Pittsburgh during the B&O strike, 1877
LIBRARY OF CONGRESS

154

The *New York Herald* called the rioters "wild beasts . . . to be shot down." At the same time a Pittsburgh grand jury called the use of troops and the shooting of strikers murder. The *Chicago Daily News* blamed the railroad owners for the strike, saying that they had operated outside the law, "plundering the roads . . . to their own enrichment."

In many instances, soldiers and militiamen who came from the ranks of the workers refused to shoot strikers. Still, the shooting went on. Thousands were injured. One hundred or more died that July.

By August, the Railway Strike of 1877 was crushed. Some workers went back to work for a pittance. Others had their previous wages restored to a living level. Still others were fired for having struck in the first place. The railroad owners formed private armies to protect their empire of tracks and cars against any such future occurrences. They also maintained private armies of goons to protect themselves from each other. Jay Gould, for example, surrounded himself constantly with armed thugs. They protected him against thugs hired by Commodore Cornelius Vanderbilt when Uncle Dan'l Drew, Gould, and Fisk were printing phony stock certificates in an effort to keep the Commodore from moving in on the Erie Railroad. State governments supported the owners by building armories in the major cities to house men and weapons in the event that troops would again be necessary to protect industry from people.

While management girded itself for more labor unrest, business began to improve. The depression of the 1870s was nearing an end. A new voice could be heard in the business community saying that the labor force in America, which consisted of the majority of citizens out of the general population of 50,000,000 people, could not be treated harshly forever if business was to survive. As far as labor was concerned, it did not intend to be dealt with so harshly in the future.

Violence continued to haunt the American worker-owner relationship all through the 1880s as labor unions sought to strengthen labor's role in the country's well-being. In 1894, violence once again broke out, this time against the Pullman Company in Chicago. George Mortimer Pullman was a builder of luxurious railroad cars. His company had declared a sizable dividend for its stockholders while cutting the pay of its workers. One hundred thousand people rioted. Again troops were mobilized, and again people died.

Most of these strikes and protests were failures in that the railroad employees did not get much satisfaction from their employers. Management simply ignored labor, and labor, in need of jobs, went back to work. Nevertheless, strong railway labor unions developed under the leadership of Eugene V. Debs, an official of the Brotherhood of Locomotive Firemen. These unions turned away from violence and sought the help of government. The government, beginning with the administration of President Grover Cleveland, wanted no further violent demonstrations that disrupted the country's well-being and also cost lives. The Cleveland administration wrote a series of investigative reports that set the foundation for future labor laws requiring a third party, a mediation board, to resolve unsettled arguments between the railroads and the rail workers, between employers and employees.

10.

Disasters

Almost as soon as steam locomotives rolled on the rails, there were accidents. At first the locomotives themselves blew up, causing the deaths of the engineers who operated them. By the late 1830s and early 1840s, whole trains derailed from time to time, which kindled public fear of the iron road. Still, the trains were not moving fast enough—20 miles per hour at the most—to cause widespread, severe passenger injury. Nor did any of the early accidents that affected passengers seem serious enough for the federal or state governments to consider the creation and regulation of safety standards. It was not until bigger, speedier, and more powerful locomotives began to appear in the 1850s that accidents on the rails became frightening disasters.

On May 6, 1853, the engineer of a Boston-bound New York, New Haven & Hartford Railroad train took his five coaches through an open drawbridge at Norwalk, Connecticut. He had failed to see a signal that the bridge was open. Two cars remained on the track; two went into the Norwalk River along with the locomotive and a baggage car. A third car teetered on the edge, broke apart, and fell into the water. Forty-six people died and 80 others were injured. Among those who died were five eminent doctors who were returning to Boston following a meeting of the American Medical Association in New York City. It was the largest loss

Earliest known photograph of an American train wreck,
Pawtucket, Rhode Island, 1856
GEORGE EASTMAN HOUSE

of life on a railroad at the time. The public began to demand safety on the rails. The state of Connecticut responded by establishing the State Board of Railroad Commissioners to create and regulate safety standards.

In the late summer of 1853, 13 people died at Valley Falls Station, Rhode Island, in a head-on collision of two trains. In July 1856, 60 people died and many more were injured in a disaster at Camp Hill, Pennsylvania. Most of the dead in that crash were church people who had boarded an unscheduled excursion train to take them to a picnic.

Eleven years after the Camp Hill Disaster, on Thursday, December 19, 1867, the "Angola Horror" shocked the nation. Forty-nine rail passengers were crushed and burned to death at Angola, New York, about 20 miles west of Buffalo. Their train, the Lake Shore & Michigan Southern Railway's *New York Express*, was bound for Buffalo. It had approached a 100-foot-long bridge on a sharp downgrade 40 feet above the frozen Big Sisters Creek. The train was

about to pass from the tracks of the Lake Shore line to those of the New York Central. As it approached the bridge, the last two cars derailed, careened across the bridge, and plunged onto the ice below. The coal stoves inside the cars burst. The resulting fires quickly reduced the wood cars to ashes, incinerating those passengers trapped in the wreckage.

An investigation concluded that the accident was caused by the lack of a standard track gauge, or width. The tracks of the New York Central, for example, like most tracks around the country, were 4 feet, 8½ inches apart. The tracks of the Lake Shore line that ran into those of the New York Central were 4 feet, 10 inches apart. In order to permit trains to make the transition from one gauge to another without stopping, "Compromise Cars" were built, whose wheels were wide enough to pass from one gauge to another. The Compromise Cars were considered as safe as any other car until the disaster at Angola.

On that cold, December day in 1867, the sixth car of the six-car Buffalo-bound *New York Express*—all Compromise Cars—slipped off the track as it passed from the 4-foot, 10-inch-wide Lake Shore track to the 4 foot, 8½-inch New York Central track. Derailed and lurching forward, it smacked the car in front of it—the fifth car—forcing it to derail and uncouple from the rest of the train.

As a result of the tragedy, the effort to standardize the gauge of all rail tracks in the United States at 4 feet, 8½ inches began, and the use of Compromise Cars was abolished.

On August 26, 1871, the *Portland Express* was on its way from Boston to Portland, Maine. But first it had to clear Everett, Massachusetts, before passing through the depot at Revere.

Everett was a junction for the Eastern Railroad of Mas-

The Angola Horror, 1867

sachusetts. Here one track, the Saugus Branch, veered off the main line and ran north a short distance through Saugus to Lynn, while the other track, the main line, ran eastward through Revere and then northward to Portland: Three trains were idling at the Everett junction on the track ahead of the *Portland Express.*

The engineer of the first train in the lineup, on its way to Saugus and Lynn, was waiting for a southbound train to pass before crossing over onto the Saugus Branch. What he did not know was that the southbound train had been held up somewhere to the north because of mechanical failure. Behind him stood the other two idling trains. And barreling behind them all came the *Portland Express.*

Eventually, the southbound train passed. And two of the three idling trains made their way to Saugus. But the third train in that procession proceeded on the main track to Revere, where it stopped to let off passengers. It was only a few minutes ahead of the *Portland Express*, which was now speeding into Revere.

By 1871, nearly every railroad line in America was equipped or being equipped with signal warning devices, a telegraph, and air brakes. However, this was not true of the Eastern Railroad of Massachusetts. Its superintendent, a crusty New Englander named Jeremiah Prescott, did not believe in modern technology or road improvements of any kind. What was good enough for the old-time originators of the line was good enough for him. The telegraph, which had been in use on the railroads of America for at least 20 years, was not worth much, according to Prescott. He relied on printed schedules that were not scrupulously followed; the whim of his train dispatchers, who worked with questionable unprinted schedules as well as the printed ones; the eyesight of his engineers; and word of mouth.

Thus were four crowded trains sent northward from Bos-

The Portland Express catastrophe, 1871
BROWN BROTHERS

ton within two and a half hours of each other on the sultry evening of August 26. There was no signal device or telegraph to warn the engineer of the first train that the southbound train was delayed due to a mechanical failure. Neither did the engineer of the *Portland Express* know that three trains had been standing still ahead of him on the main line at Everett; that two had moved on; and that the third was dangerously close ahead.

When the *Portland Express* approached the fatal moment, the hot, dark, August night had been misted by a light fog that had crept in from the sea. The two red lanterns on the rear of the train that was stopped at Revere were now dim and ghostlike ahead. By the time the engineer of the *Portland Express* saw them and realized he could not set his brakes fast enough, it was too late. The *Portland Express* slammed into the train at the Revere station. Twenty-nine passengers died. Fifty-seven were injured.

The Revere Disaster caused an outcry all over New England. "Deliberate murder," cried prominent New Englander Wendell Phillips, who spoke at public rallies protesting railroad operation in Massachusetts, singling out the management of the Eastern. Charles F. Adams, Massachusetts Commissioner of Railroads, asserted that "a simple message to the branch lines . . . would have solved the difficulty."

As a result of an investigation of the Revere Disaster, Superintendent Jeremiah Prescott lost his position, becoming an assistant to a new man who installed telegraphic communications on the line and employed dispatchers who knew how to run trains by telegraphing train schedules and train locations en route. In addition, all rail lines in Massachusetts that did not modernize the running of their trains with telegraphy were ordered to do so. The Eastern never fully recovered from the disaster. Legal action against the railroad, together with accusations of corruption, plagued the line until it was absorbed by the Boston & Maine in 1884.

The Lake Shore & Michigan was in another horrendous accident only nine years after the Angola Horror. This one stunned the nation and was forever called the Ashtabula Catastrophe. Early in the evening of December 29, 1876, the 11-car *Pacific Express* pulled by two locomotives puffed out of Ashtabula, Ohio, heading west. As it crossed the 165-foot bridge high over Ashtabula Creek, the bridge collapsed. The entire train plunged into the creek, killing 34 people and injuring many more.

On August 10, 1887, still another horrible rail tragedy stunned the nation. Two engines pulling 15 cars of the Toledo, Peoria & Western Railroad, jammed with sightseers, were heading for Niagara Falls, New York. The train rolled onto a bridge that collapsed under it. The first locomotive somehow made it across. The other locomotive went into the water, taking all 15 cars behind it. Eighty-four people drowned or burned to death in the wreckage.

Not all train wrecks were caused by poor management, human error, badly designed and maintained bridges, faulty equipment, or even robbers. One famous wreck was produced for the sport of it—and for the money to be gained from those who would pay admission to see such a catastrophe.

An ambitious ticket agent, William George Crush, convinced his bosses, the owners of the Missouri, Kansas & Texas Railroad—nicknamed the Katy—that they could make their railroad famous and make a lot of money, too, by staging a railroad crash. With a lot of ballyhoo—advertising, newspaper stories, posters—Crush also convinced between 30,000 and 40,000 people to come, pay for, and witness the event. The scene was set near Waco, Texas. Crush established a tent city that he named for himself—Crush City. He provided food and drink for the audience. It took an army of sheriff's deputies to move the huge crowd back from the rails.

On September 15, 1896, two locomotives, one painted green, the other red, and each pulling six passenger coaches, backed off a mile. On a signal from Crush—a wave of his hat—the engineers and firemen driving the empty trains jumped off as the two locomotives headed for each other at 60 miles an hour. A minute later they smashed into each other in a tremendous explosion that hurtled hot metal, wood chunks, and live steam at the throng. Two people died. Many were injured. One of two photographers at the scene, J. C. Deane, lost his eye when it was hit by a flying bolt. But he stuck to his camera and photographed

Aftermath of staged wreck at Crush City, Texas, 1896

the wreck. He was thereafter known as Joe "One-Eye" Deane. The great crowd cheered the impact and roared its approval as it picked over the smoldering wreck, looking for souvenirs.

One line, the Illinois Central, founded in the 1850s and destined for a legendary place in American history, ran north and south between Chicago and New Orleans. On the night of April 30, 1900, one of the Illinois Central's best engineers, John Luther "Casey" Jones, unavoidably rammed his *Cannonball Express* at more than 100 miles an hour into a freight train that had stalled near Canton, Mississippi.

Casey died instantly in the twisted wreckage of his once magnificent iron horse, Locomotive No. 382. The steam engine had been a powerhouse marvel. Although the crash cost him his life, Casey Jones's quick action and braking skill prevented a far worse accident and any additional loss of life. He could have jumped as he ordered his fireman, Sim Webb, to do. Webb lived. But Casey hung on and earned himself an eternal niche in American folklore and song:

"Come all you rounders if you want to hear
The story told about a brave engineer.
Casey Jones was the rounder's name,
On a big eight wheeler, boys, he won his fame."

Wreck in Calvary, Kentucky, 1900
SMITHSONIAN INSTITUTION

11.

Locomotives, Cars, and Progress

Were it not for the mechanical ingenuity of the industrial nineteenth-century American, no amount of financial wizardry and manipulation could have produced that wonder of wonders, the iron horse, the fire-breathing, earth-shaking, monster builder of an "empire and an epic" that took America where she wanted to go most of all—west!

Not long after Horatio Allen had designed the *Best Friend of Charleston* in 1830, he designed another locomotive, the South Carolina, whose wheels were flexible, or swivel trucks—sets of wheels encased in a framework—that moved for the first time with the curve of a track to keep heavy locomotives and coaches from derailing.

Rail tracks in England were usually straight and very gently curved. English locomotive and car wheels that had rigid axles that did not shift position around a curve did not derail. American rail tracks, on the other hand, followed a more varied terrain and were more sharply curved. American trains with fixed wheels chugging around a sharp curve would topple over. Allen's swivel truck idea kept locomotives and coaches on the tracks around sharp curves. It became standard on all American and, later, on English railroads as well.

Not all the credit for flexible trucks went to Horatio Allen, however. In 1831, unaware of Allen's improvement,

John B. Jervis, a mechanic for the Mohawk & Hudson Railway, designed an improved swivel truck for the line's locomotives. At about the same time Ross Winans, a builder of coaches and later, locomotives, secured a patent for a further improvement on Horatio Allen's idea of a swivel truck.

Also in 1831, Matthias William Baldwin, a New Jersey-born Philadelphia jeweler and bookbinder, built a small experimental steam locomotive and ran it on a circular track. The Philadelphia, Germantown & Norristown Railroad Company was so impressed with Baldwin's engine that they hired him for the sum of $4,000 to build a bigger one for their tracks. They had in mind to change their railroad from horse-drawn power to steam power.

A year later, Baldwin and his mechanics unveiled a steam locomotive called *Old Ironsides*. *Old Ironsides* was made of iron and wood. Its top speed was about 28 miles an hour with power enough to pull 30 tons in rain or shine. The

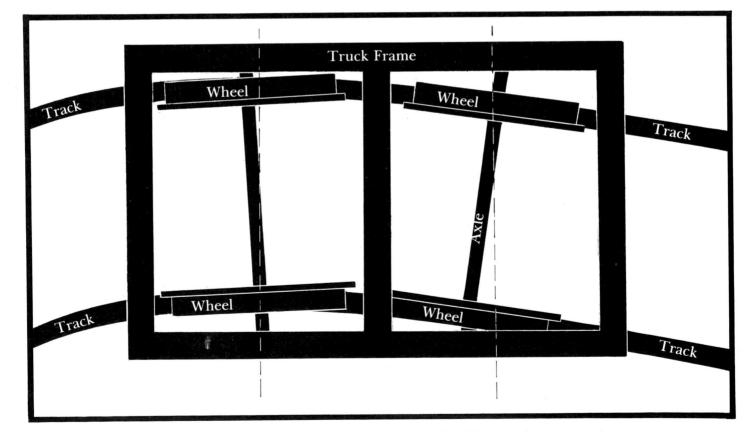

Diagram of a swivel truck showing position of flexible wheels on rounding a curb
LEONARD EVERETT FISHER

Philadelphia, Germantown & Norristown Railroad, however, claimed that the engine was inadequate in rainy weather. The company refused to pay Baldwin the entire amount of money due him. Steam-powered passenger trains left Philadelphia on fair-weather days. But horses pulled freight and passengers along the rails on rainy days.

Matthias William Baldwin and his mechanics built more locomotives than anyone else. During his own lifetime, Baldwin put 1,500 steam locomotives on American rails. The company he founded in 1854 with Matthew Baird, the Baldwin Locomotive Works, went on, after his death in 1866, to produce more than 60,000 locomotives. But more important than Baldwin's energy and engineering skill were the constant improvements he and others made on the locomotives that contributed to the quick and stunning growth of the railroad industry in America.

Isaac Dripps, a mechanic who worked for Robert L. Stevens, president of the Camden & Amboy Railroad during the early 1860s, contributed to many of the improvements. Dripps introduced the bell and oil-burning headlamp on the locomotive. He was also responsible for the cowcatcher, the protruding angular iron grate at the head of the engine used to nudge animals off the track.

Improvements were made on the locomotive's smokestack. Numerous smokestacks were designed with or without flared shapes to reduce the shower of sparks that fell on the locomotive and the cars behind. These were also designed to prevent the sparks from igniting the countryside through which the train passed. Coal-burning locomotives used stacks called Diamonds, Shotguns, Capstacks, and Congdons. Wood-burning locomotives also used Diamonds in addition to Sunflowers and Balloons.

By the 1840s, a weatherproof cab enclosed the engineer and fireman. The cab, mounted on the engine, permitted

Smokestacks
LEONARD EVERETT FISHER

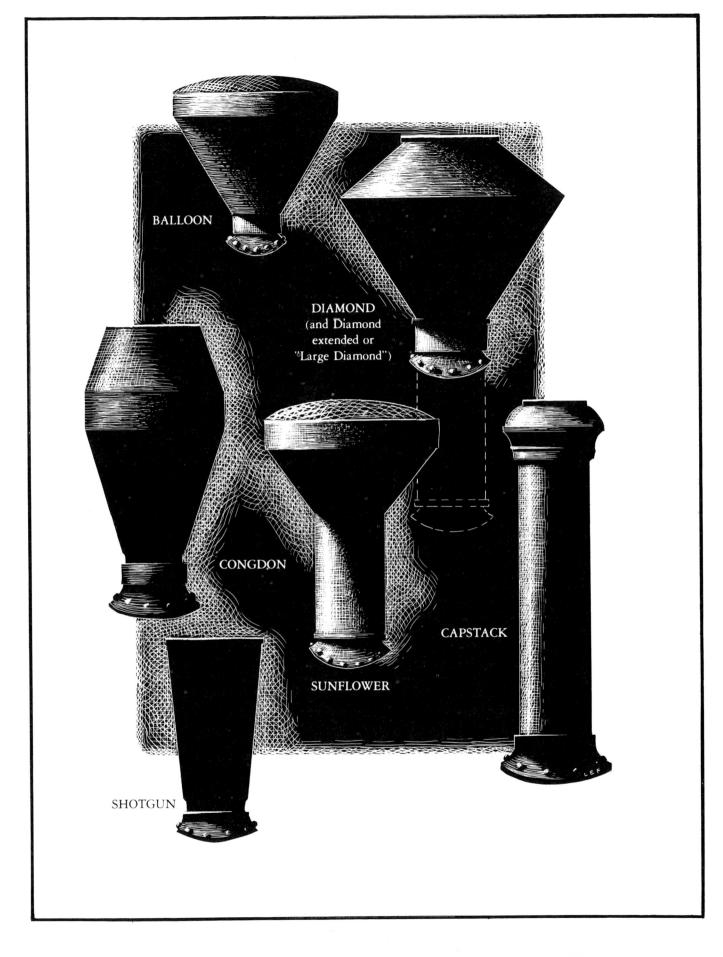

BALLOON

DIAMOND
(and Diamond
extended or
"Large Diamond")

CONGDON

SUNFLOWER

CAPSTACK

SHOTGUN

the crew to operate the locomotive in comfort, out of the weather. Also, whale oil for headlamps was replaced by kerosene, a brighter-burning fluid that made night travel safer. By 1881, locomotives would have electric headlamps.

Besides the locomotives, the caboose was the one car that seemed to capture the imagination of every fancier of the iron road. It was the rocking inner sanctum—the clubhouse—of the crew, or so it seemed. Officially it was the office of the conductor and the quarters of the train workers. It was where they ate, slept, kept their trip records and reports, locked away cash and valuables in iron safes, and spent their idle hours rolling along on the end of the train.

Much different than the caboose was George Mortimer Pullman's *Palace Sleeping Car*. Especially built for the new transcontinental railroad era, Pullman's *Palace Sleeping Car* offered luxurious service to the well-to-do. By 1864, Pullman had developed a comfortable arrangement for train

Railroad caboose in Grand Island, Nebraska, 1898
UNION PACIFIC RAILROAD MUSEUM

The first Pullman *Palace Sleeping Car*, 1859
ASSOCIATION OF AMERICAN RAILROADS

sleeping: a highly upholstered hinged upper berth that could be let down as a bed at night or pulled up out of the way in the morning. He produced the "vestibule car," which enclosed the outside-car platforms, creating a bellowslike tunnel between two cars so that passage from one car to another could be safely made. His company designed an ornate "hotel car" in 1869, in which one could ride, eat, sleep, and relax. The hotel car later became the "parlor car," an overly decorative space on wheels in which to relax. His plush dining cars, which appeared in the 1870s, offered gourmet dining in rich surroundings of hand-carved woods, velvet draperies, and crystal chandeliers. There, sumptuous meals fit for royalty were cooked by Pullman's black chefs on board and served by Pullman's waiters, not all of whom were black.

Unlike the Pullman cars, the "Zulu" cars that took the not-so-well-to-do immigrants west were hardly luxurious or plush. No one knows how the Zulu cars got their name. Every immigrant who ever rode west in a leaky, springless Zulu knew that it took an extraordinary will and constitution to survive the crowded, body-aching ride across America. Those who rode in the rear cars had the worst of the jerking and rocking motion of the train. Those up front had a smoother ride. The accommodations were divided into three groupings: single men traveled in one car, regardless of ethnic origin or nationality; families and single women traveled in the second car; a third car was reserved for Chinese workers going west to work on the railroad.

173

Zulu car

Sometimes the trains were so crowded that a number of single men traveled with families and single women. On other crowded occasions a few Chinese found themselves in the single-men car.

The thousands of immigrants who traveled in the Zulu cars had little choice. Most were too poor to afford more comfortable transportation. What little money they had bought them space in a Zulu car. Those without any money at all had their Zulu transportation paid for by the railroad, provided they went west either to colonize farmland owned by the railroad or to work on the railroad itself.

In 1879, penniless, lovesick Robert Louis Stevenson, the Scottish author who would soon write *Dr. Jekyll and Mr. Hyde* and *Treasure Island,* took a Zulu train from New York to San Francisco to marry a young lady he had met in Europe. His family did not approve of his marital aims and had cut off his funds.

Parlor car interior

Calling himself an "amateur immigrant," the frail, courageous 29-year-old Stevenson described a Zulu car in his 1892 book *Across the Plains* as being a "long narrow wooden box, like a flat-roofed Noah's ark . . . where there is scarce elbow room for two to sit . . . [and] no space enough for one to lie." The trip west for Stevenson was as depressing as it was miserable. "Civility is the main comfort that you miss," Stevenson wrote. "Equality, though conceived very largely in America, does not extend so low down as to an emigrant."

The interior of the early Zulu car was made of rough boards from floor to ceiling. Narrow wood benches extended down the length of the car, lined up on each side of a center aisle. The benches themselves were straight-backed, uncushioned boards. The backs could be adjusted so pairs of benches faced each other. Beds were nothing more than wood boards laid across these facing seats. A lumpy straw cushion or mattress could be purchased to ease the journey.

On a higher level there were fixed cubicles or adjustable wood palettes, which could be raised or lowered by a chain. A passenger and his family could crawl into one of these upper spaces, which cost a few dollars more than the seats below, and enjoy some nighttime privacy. Food was either eaten at trackside dining halls during 20-minute stops or bought en route from "news butchers," who also sold soap, towels, and sundries. Breakfast, lunch, and dinner, when not eaten "out" on one of the stops, was cooked on the pot-bellied stoves in each of the cars. The stoves were the best place to brew coffee.

Dangerous oil lamps lit the rocking car at night and posed a constant threat of fire. Most of the Zulus had a "convenience room," an unsanitary, closetlike latrine at one end of the car. The overcrowded cars were either freezing or suffocatingly hot, depending on the season. Nearly everyone traveling the Zulus was afflicted with itchy body rashes, and tempers flared.

Some of the tired and fearful immigrants became sick with influenza, diarrhea, and other ailments. Stevenson described one of the passengers in his car as a "little boy of eight or nine who had the whooping cough." Stevenson, who did not enjoy good health in the best of times, was himself sick for a while.

When the stale-aired cars reached the end of the line and discharged their passengers, their filthy interiors were hosed down. As time went on, the hardness of the Zulu car was softened by better-cushioned seats and better-cushioned sleeping berths and improved trackside dining. The trip west, however less harsh, still jarred body and soul.

Stevenson wrote:

> When I think how the railroad has been pushed through this unwatered wilderness and haunt of savage tribes and now will bear an emigrant . . . from the Atlantic to the Golden Gates, . . . how at each stage of the construction, roaring, impromptu cities full of gold and lust and death, sprang up and . . . died away, . . . how in these uncouth places pigtailed Chinese pirates worked side by side with border ruffians and broken men from Europe . . . gambling, drinking, quarrelling and murdering like wolves, . . . I go on to remember that all this epical turmoil was conducted by gentlemen in frocked coats . . . with a view to nothing more extraordinary than a fortune and a . . . visit to Paris.

Human cargo moving west to settle the land was not as well accommodated as the food being moved east. William Davis, a fish dealer, had packed a freight car with ice and filled it with fish caught in the Great Lakes. He shipped the load to

Detroit. William H. Hammond, a Chicago meat dealer, also used ice to preserve meat for long-distance shipment. In 1867, Hammond packed a car with ice and meat and shipped it off to Boston. The meat arrived cold but in a deteriorated condition. The problem was that the air cooled by the ice did not circulate evenly through the car. Also, the car allowed outside heat to enter.

The solution was first provided by Joel Tiffany in 1868 when he designed heat-proof car doors and placed the ice in containers. Over the next 15 or 20 years a number of patents to improve the refrigerator car were filed with the U.S. government. By 1877, a vastly improved refrigerator car, or "reefer," was a regular fixture on the rails between the stockyards of Chicago and the markets of New York, Boston, and Philadelphia. The cars were also used to ship perishable fruits and vegetables from farm areas to big city markets anywhere in the country.

In 1869, one year after Tiffany's innovative refrigerator car design had been introduced, 23-year-old George West-inghouse invented air brakes for locomotives. Three years earlier he had invented both a machine for putting derailed cars back on their tracks and a "frog," which enabled a moving train to slide from one track onto another.

Westinghouse was introduced to mechanical devices early in his life. His father owned a machine shop in upstate New York, where young George spent his days tinkering. He served in the Union army during the Civil War, after which he briefly attended Union College in Schenectady, New York.

Westinghouse's air brakes allowed more sudden stopping, thus reducing the risk of collisions. Yet although some rail-roads installed the brakes, others did not. Finally, in 1893, the federal government made air brakes mandatory on all locomotives. Westinghouse went on to invent safety signals

George Westinghouse
WESTINGHOUSE ELECTRIC CORPORATION

and other railroad devices. He was also responsible for introducing alternating current to America, a system of electric current invented by a Croatian-American scientist, Nikola Tesla. Alternating current was a less expensive system than Thomas Alva Edison's direct current and helped make it possible to bring cheap electricity into many American households. George Westinghouse, who held some 400 patents at the time of his death in 1914, founded the Westinghouse Electric Company in 1886. The company grew to become the world's largest manufacturer of electric-powered machinery.

In 1873, Eli Janney patented an automatic coupler that allowed the switchman to stand free of the "knuckle" mechanism. The switchman no longer had to risk his life and limbs by getting between the cars. The railroad owners resisted the change since, in all probability, it would have been too expensive to install them on the thousands of rolling stock then in operation. Switchmen went on losing their fingers, hands, and lives until 20 years later, in 1893, when the government forced the railroads to install automatic couplers on all trains.

Another improvement that became indispensable to the running of a railroad was the telegraph. On May 24, 1844, after years of struggle and disappointment, Samuel Finley Breese Morse successfully tested the telegraph on a wire strung from the U.S. Supreme Court in Washington, D.C., to Baltimore, Maryland. The message he tapped out, "What hath God wrought," ushered in the modern era of communication.

Morse was an 1810 graduate of Yale College, where he excelled in art and electrical experiments. Upon graduation, he gave up his interest in electricity to become a successful artist, both in England and the United States. In 1826, he founded the National Academy of Design in New

York City and became its first president. His 1825 portrait of the Marquis de Lafayette hangs in New York's City Hall. It was aboard the *Sully* on an ocean crossing between England and America in 1832 that Samuel F. B. Morse's interest in electricity was rekindled. He learned in idle conversation that electricity could be almost instantly sent through a wire to any distance. Hearing this, he conceived of sending electrical impulses—messages—through a wire before the *Sully* made port. In 1851, Charles Minot of the Erie began using the telegraph to run his railroad. By the late 1850s, Morse's telegraph was in widespread use, directing the movement of trains.

An innovation that was born as much out of necessity as any mechanical device was standard time. Before 1883, nearly every city, town, and village in the United States seemed to operate on its own time. They called it local or sun time. There was great confusion, especially in trying to keep connecting train schedules. Trains arriving at the same time at the same station from different regions all operated on different times. No one could maintain a reliable schedule or expect to know the exact time even if he or she just walked from one town to another.

For example, 12 o'clock noon on Staten Island in New York City could be 12:30 in the afternoon in Brooklyn, only four miles away across Lower New York Bay. At the same time, clocks in Hoboken, New Jersey, a few miles north, might be reading 11:45 in the morning. Across the Hudson River in Manhattan the time at that very moment might be 12:15 in the afternoon. It might also be 12:15 in the afternoon in Chicago, even though the sun in its westward course was at least an hour later in reaching Chicago. The fact was that no one knew exactly what time it was anywhere.

In 1883, the railroads adopted a method of standard time that all agreed to follow. They set up vertical time zones across the country that more or less kept time with the sun's westward course. Cities like New York, Trenton, Philadelphia, Wilmington, Baltimore, and Washington, D.C., which fell in the same eastern time zone, would all have the same time. Twelve o'clock noon in New York would be 12 o'clock noon in Baltimore. Chicago and all the cities in its time zone would be an hour earlier. San Francisco on the west coast and all the cities in its time zone would be three hours earlier.

A year later, an international conference was held in Washington, D.C., to adopt a worldwide standard time system. Although no agreement was reached, the delegates did decide to make the meridian that passes through Greenwich, England, the line from which world standard time would be established. Eventually, standard time based on the Greenwich meridian was adopted by every nation in the world.

Progressive locomotive and car design, together with applied railroad engineering, practical science, and the inventive mind, so refined the operation of American railroads that railroading, considered to be a dangerous business earlier in the 19th century, was no longer thought to be particularly hazardous by the end of the century. If there were hazards, they were caused largely by greedy management and investors who thought more of their profits than the safety of the rails.

12.

The Way It Was to Be

Despite the turmoil and corruption present in a nation that had changed so fast from its modest roots, America and her railroads pressed on. By the end of the 1800s, America was a new and larger country that stretched from the Atlantic to the Pacific, from the Gulf of Mexico to the Great Lakes, all tied together by railroads. America was a new spirit riding to glory on a railroad.

The big engines lived up to John Stevens's early prophecy of traveling at speeds of 100 miles per hour. Although Stevens did not live to see the truth of his prediction, one of his contemporaries did. Horatio Allen, the engineer who brought the *Stourbridge Lion* from England in 1829, lived to see the transcontinental streak across the plains in 1890 at nearly 100 miles an hour.

Many like New England's singular author, Henry David Thoreau, who thought little of mechanized societies and the railroad in particular, finally had to come to terms with the inevitable rush of civilization.

Expressing his dislike for railroads chiefly because the Fitchburg Railroad—later to become the Boston & Maine—skirted too close to the edge of his Walden Pond, Thoreau wrote in 1854:

We do not ride the railroad; it rides upon us. Did you

ever think what those sleepers are that underlie the railroad? Each one is a man, an Irishman, or a Yankee man. The rails are laid on them.

Later he would write:

When I hear the iron horse make the hills echo with his snort like thunder, . . . it seems as if the earth had got a race now worthy to inhabit it.

A steam engine in Spanish Fork Canyon, Utah.
Photograph by Richard Steinheimer, 1951

Selected Bibliography

Asher & Adams. *Pictorial Album of American Industry*. New York: Asher & Adams, 1876; New York: Rutledge, 1976.

Backmun, Ora. *Western North Carolina: Its Mountains and Its People to 1880*. Boone, Ky.: Appalachian Consortium Press, 1977.

Beebe, Lucius, and Charles Clegg. *Hear the Train Blow*. New York: Dutton, 1952.

Boni, Margaret Bradford, ed. *Fireside Book of Folk Songs*. New York: Simon & Schuster, 1947.

Briggs, Asa. *The Nineteenth Century*. London: Thames & Hudson, 1970.

Brown, Dee. *Hear That Lonesome Whistle Blow*. New York: Holt, Rinehart & Winston, 1947.

Dickens, Charles. *American Notes*. London: Chapman and Hall, 1842.

Dodge, Grenville M. *How We Built the Union Pacific Railroad*. Washington, D.C.: U.S. Government Printing Office, 1910.

Fisher, Leonard Everett. *Nineteenth Century America*. Vol. 7, *The Unions*. New York: Holiday House, 1982.

Freedman, Russell. *Indian Chiefs*. New York: Holiday House, 1987.

Freedman, Russell. *Buffalo Hunt*. New York: Holiday House, 1988.

Gardner, Alexander. *Photographic Sketch Book of the Civil War*, vols. 1 and 2. Washington, D.C.: Philips & Solomons, 1866; New York: Dover, 1959.

Hastings, Paul. *Railroads: An International History*. New York: Praeger, 1972.

Holbrook, Stewart H. *The Story of the American Railroad*. New York: Crown, 1947.

Horan, James D. *Mathew Brady*. New York: Crown, 1955.

Jensen, Oliver. *History of Railroads in America*. New York: American Heritage, 19

Kennedy, Ludovic. *A Book of Railway Journeys*. New York: Rawson, Wade, 1980.

Kundhardt, D. M., and P. B. Kundhardt. *Twenty Days*. New York: Castle, 1965.

La Farge, Oliver. *A Pictorial History of the American Indian*. New York: Crown, 1957.

Latrobe, John Hazelhurst Boneval. *The Baltimore and Ohio Railroad: Personal Recollections*. Baltimore, 1868, 12–18 *passim* in Hart, Albert Bushnell, ed. *American History Told by Contemporaries*, vol. 3. New York: Macmillan, 1968.

McCready, Albert L. *Railroads in the Days of Steam*. New York: American Heritage, 1960.

McKissack, Patricia, and Frederick McKissack. *A Long Hard Journey*. New York: Walker, 1989.

Moody, John. *The Railroad Builders*. New Haven: Yale University Press, 1919.

Schmitt, Martin F., and Dee Brown. *Fighting Indians of the West*. New York: Bonanza, 1958.

Severson, Thor. *Sacramento: An Illustrated History, 1839–1874*. Sacramento: California Historical Society, 1973.

Stevenson, Robert Louis. *Across the Plains*. New York: Scribner, 1892; London: Chatto & Windus, 1892.

Swerdlow, Joel L. "The Erie Canal/Living Link to Our Past," *National Geographic*, 178 (Nov. 1990): 38–65.

Ward, James A. *Railroads and the Character of America, 1820–1887*. Knoxville: University of Tennessee, 1986.

Wheeler, Keith. *The Railroaders*. New York: Time-Life, 1973.

Wilson, Mitchell. *American Science and Invention*. New York: Simon & Schuster, 1954.

Wilson, Woodrow. *A History of the American People*. Vol. 4, *Critical Changes and Civil War;* vol. 5, *Reunion and Nationalization*. New York: Harper & Brothers, 1901.

Index

Italicized numbers indicate pages with photos.